Marlene Dumas

Sweet Nothings

Notes and Texts

edited by Mariska van den Berg

First edition published by Marlene Dumas, Galerie Paul Andriesse and De Balie Publishers, 1998
Second edition [revised and expanded] published by Koenig Books, London 2014
and D.A.P./Distributed Art Publishers Inc. 2015

I keep repeating what he said and what he said and what she said and what I said.
I cannot look at anything without thinking about what he said and what she said and what I said.

There is nothing more terrible than having a good 'talk' with someone
Erik Andriesse

Contents

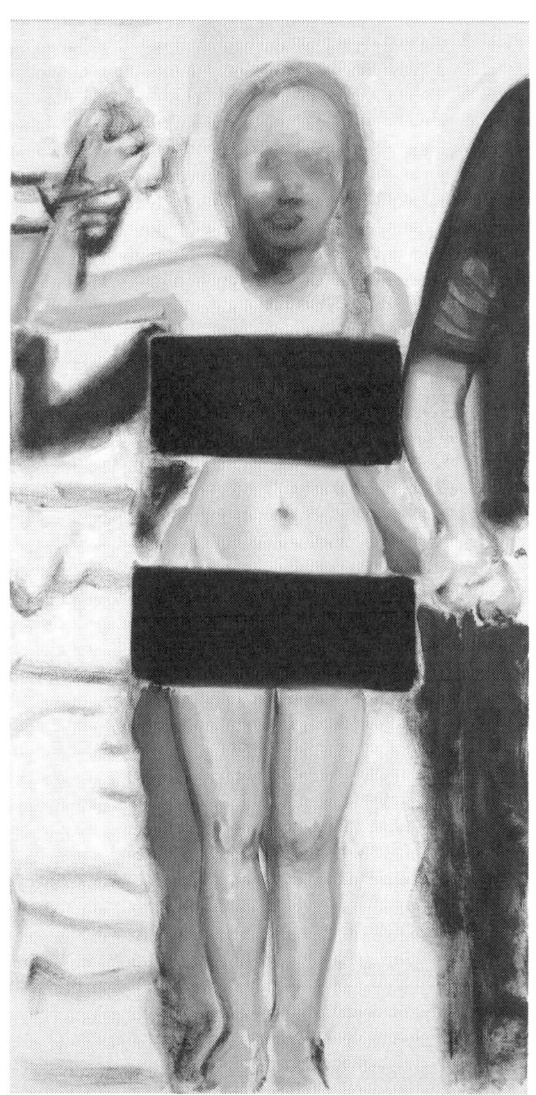

Woman of Algiers 2001 200 x 100 cm

Introduction

Marlene Dumas has a remarkable affinity for language and from the very beginning writing has played an important part in her work as a visual artist. She made use of text in her earliest collages and still writes short sentences directly onto her drawings. Her individual works and exhibitions are given intriguing and revealing titles, such as *The Eyes of the Night Creatures*, *Miss Interpreted*, and more recently *Measuring your own Grave* and *The Image as Burden*. Over the last thirty years, she has written an impressive number of texts ranging from aphorisms, statements and short poetic pieces to longer analytical essays. These writings focus on her own work – tackling aspects such as subject matter, background and sources – as well as its reception, her position as an artist and the nature of art and painting in a more general sense. *Sweet Nothings* – now in a revised and enlarged edition – provides a selection of her best and most representative writings.

An important motivation to write, as she makes clear in her text *Why do I write (about Art)*[1] – is a strong desire to speak for herself. If an artwork does not contain all the necessary information within itself – and it does not, she says - then discussion is of vital importance to its contextualization. In this discussion she wants to speak for herself, not to avoid misunderstanding as she believes there is 'no correct interpretation' of her work, but 'interpretations can be more or less creative'[2]. As readings of her work can even be influenced by the 'cheap politically correct principles' she intends to question in her work, she wishes to contribute to the (politics of) interpretation herself, at least to refine her own confusions and contradictions. 'I write to participate in the writing of my own history' she once wrote. Paradoxically Dumas' texts themselves rarely provide any answers. They do reflect some of her intentions and in that sense they are informative, but they leave the ambiguity of the artwork untouched. This ambiguity however, is far from noncommittal, being targeted instead at creating space for a myriad of meanings, although this does not allow every interpretation.

As a collection of her writings, *Sweet Nothings* also reflects Dumas' preference for the written rather than the spoken word. One of her earliest books was entitled *No interviews Please* (1987), and in *No more Interviews*, written in the same year, she gives her reasons for objecting to the verbal interview. For although she still gives them – albeit rarely – the interaction with language and the greater space for reflection which distinguishes the written from the spoken word, is essential to her.

Marlene Dumas has an entirely individual voice, which in no way conforms to the usual way of writing about art. The tone of her writings is personal, colored by emotion and a relativizing, sometimes sardonic, sense of humor, reflecting on the complexity of the human condition and the often problematic inter-human communications. 'If you really want to talk to others, get a good translator', she writes[3]. She uses words and forms of address from everyday speech, often confronting the reader directly in the 'I' or 'you' form. Where in her art she starts working from existing images, in her writing she draws on existing literary forms. When writing about love, she plays with cryptic and teasing sayings, the love letter or poem, all as a means of finally saying something about art. In her own words she uses 'all the cheap tricks' to attract attention and confront the observer directly[4], yet actually as a beginning.

For the reading of her artworks the movement of her hand and the materiality of her medium are as important as the subjects she chooses. Similarly in her writings she relishes the substance of language. Enjoying the interplay between the meaning of a word, the sound of it and the sequential rhythm when poetically strung together, she is aiming for 'sentences with sex appeal' and 'the intoxication of rhythmic rhetorical arousal'.[5] The content of many texts is hallmarked with clichés and stereotypes – such as 'the model' or 'the suspect' – that are questioned and invalidated. The same holds true of the more abstract concepts that she brings into play. Although all-embracing concepts such as love, evil or identity are unwieldy, Dumas manages to subtly articulate and expand them, and to bring them back to a more personal level of experience, which also accommodates complexity, doubt and nuance.

Marlene Dumas plays upon an illusion of intimacy and a suggestion of narrative, without redeeming the promise, because 'there is ambiguousness to come to terms with'[6]. Highly commended as her texts may be by many, she chooses to present them as *Sweet Nothings*.

Mariska van den Berg

1 *Why do I write (about Art)*, 1992, p. 11

2 From an unpublished letter to W. Welling, 1988.

3 From *The Hatred of Others*, 1994, p. 89

4 From *The perfect Lover, the absent Lover and the Daughter*, 1996, p. 106

5 Ibid. noot 1

6 Ibid. noot 1

Why do I write (about Art)

I write about art because I am a believer.
I believe
in the power
of words
especially the
WRITTEN WORD.

I have seen the glory and the power of the word.
I have experienced the power of repetition,
the intoxication of rythmic rhetorical arousal.

I write because I love words.
Or rather, what is more erotic than a body with sex appeal?
A sentence with sex appeal.

I write because I enjoy writing.
I write about art because it supplies a (safe) context. It is a privilege to be able to read and to be read. What a pleasure to have conversations with human beings (dead and alive) without having to see them.

I write because I instinctively respond to the already written.
I am affected by the LAW. The LAW is already written. Being from South-Africa, you know that a comma or a bracket, more or less, can cost a person's life. A good lawyer (an interpreter of the law) is essential for survival. You don't have to respect it, but you have to know its loopholes in order to escape it: or remake it.

I want to grow up, stand up, even though I prefer to lie down
(I write lying down).

I write about my own work because I want to speak for myself.
I might not be the only authority, nor the best authority, but I want to participate in the writing of my own history. Why should artists be validated by outside authorities. I don't like being paternalised and colonialised by every Tom, Dick or Harry that comes along (male or female).

The overexposure of 'Meaning' and its mistreatment.
It is not a fear of being 'misunderstood' that drives me to write (not anymore). 'Meaning' and 'Mis-understanding' are not that useful as terms to describe visual issues. De- and re- contextualisations are part and parcel of creative experiences.

Even Duchamp mentioned the relationship between the 'unexpressed but intended and the unintentionally expressed'. Seeing that the so-called passive spectator has disappeared, we are stuck with (over)active collaborators, finishing off the artworks. Accepting freedom of speech, that is inevitable. But it is a question of distinguishing between who says what (and to the benefit of whom?). Critics should not adhere to the intentional fallacy in reverse – playing Freud to reveal my true intentions to me. Artwork is not synonymous to intention. It is peculiar that although almost everybody says that artworks don't give answers, they seem to be sure that a good work asks questions. It sounds like the other side of the same coin to me. What artworks do, the roles they can or do still play in our society, is unclear to me. Writing about art refines my own confusions and contradictions about these matters.

I write because I am amused by the politics of interpretation.
'In the beginning was the word
and the word became flesh
and it never healed' – Breyten Breytenbach.
In the beginning comes the description containing the prescription
and the unacknowledged prejudice.
– I said that. (?!)

Persistent misconceptions and the intimidating and oppressive (mis)use of theory. As an artstudent I was offended by the expression 'as stupid as a painter'. Painters seemed incapable of any serious critique of their own assumptions (they still do). Yet theorising that has been seen as the criterion for intelligence has been challenged by many. Marguerite Duras: 'It has been under attack for centuries. It ought to be crushed by now and it should lose itself in a re-awakening of the senses, blind itself and be still'. There are more ways to write than the human mind can conceive of. I'd like to paint lovesongs and write like a rapsong...

I write about art because I want to dissociate myself from the tone of most art-writings. I am not impressed by ART neither disappointed, because I never believed in ART as the Big White Hope anyway; or saw artists as larger than life.

a) I don't like pompous, purple prose; rather give me a cruel, cold text, with a touch of evil and a hand full of salt to rub in the wounds.

b) No dull, pedantic, well-mannered academicism. Art does not originate in a clean, linear way. Why try to describe it in such a way. David Hammons once said that he did not care much for the art audience. They were over-educated and never had any fun.

c) No shortsighted oppositional writing accompanying cheap politically correct principles. I like short texts, but condensation is not the same as oversimplification. E.g. since poor old Modernism (equated with formalism) has become the Nazi's of recent art history, everyone has to throw a stone in that direction; from their glasshouses.

The notion of 'the Relevant'.
At certain times only certain aspects are stressed and others repressed. Certain artists works are ignored on the basis that they are dealing with issues that are ir-relevant to our times, as if what is described as being of the past has and could ever be resolved. (As if there were no life after death.) This is most often done by the same authorities that pretend to dismiss linear thinking. For me the past is always present, even though I don't know anything about most of it. E.g. Jesus is still the most erotic male image in painting today.

I write about art not to promote, defend or explain the work, but rather as an apology. Since I participate in 'the Artworld' I have felt ashamed. (Shame is the Cinderella of the unpleasant emotions, having received much less attention than anxiety, guilt and depression! And I'm definitely not a melancholic!) Recognition by those you feel ambivalent towards is unhealthy and feeds feelings of insignificance. I write because I am screening my own inconsistencies.

To write or not to write.
I like to read about art. It also stimulates me to go and do something totally different in the middle of a sentence, or afterwards, like picking up a paintbrush for example. It is only that due to the overload of art historians, artists and other artrelated people, we are floaded by an overload of insipid writings, to such an extent that when you get to the right thing, you are too tired to read it.

Some Qualities I exhibit

Indirectness, lack of
freedom, unfaithfulness and fragility...
Is commentary useful? I say yes.
Is not all the necessary information
contained in the work itself? I say no.
It is largely contained outside
the work.

One can, one does [I do] and
one has to, at times, put words
into the mouth of the work,
and/or take them out again.
One's eyes are situated next
to one's ears.

I have often thought of my work as
images of lamentation [elegies].
I have sometimes thought of it as
displays of unnecessary sentimentalism.
And
I also realize that artists, like
semiologists, always tend to
'betray facts for a good phrase'.

eople are often confused and are sometimes even killed by doing the wrong thing in the wrong place.

BACKGROUND.

NAME: MARLENE DUMAS
1953–1976 SOUTH AFRICA.
1976 → HOLLAND.

THE WORD

••• Thou shalt have no other gods before me
Thou shalt not make unto thee any graven image
or any likeness or anything that is in heaven
above or that is in the earth beneath or that
is in the waters under the earth •••

THE FLESH

In the beginning was the word
and the word became flesh
and it never healed —(Breyten Breytenbach.)

THE LAW.

Diana was a wit noi
Martin was a bryn boy
dey fell in love
dey fell in love
dey fell in love

sê Diana se mense
what about de lô
sê Martin se mense
what abou' de lô
sê almal die mense
what abou' de lô

sê Martin sê Diana
watte lô
God's lô
Man's lô
devils lô
watte lô

sê die mense net
de lô
de lô
de lô
de lô

—(Adam Small)

TIME 16:35:47 ELV. 00.1' dR=1.20KM dAZ=1.19KM SM=100225'
ST 10 RS 10 HT 00.3 NA 003 SF 30 TD 08 DA 139

produce a pattern of arrows that show where storms may be forming.

THE TALES

Mermaids
have no soul
No death
but if they cry
they die

A WOMAN
has neither paradise
nor hel to go to
If she dies
Nothing is left of
her.
—(Islam)

Too Much Beauty
May attract the
evil eye. Parents
were once known
to disfure especially
pretty babies in
order to protect th
(people and ghost
have no set form.
They take on whatev
form they choose.
I live in perpetual
doubt of how to
act towards them

THE CONFLICT.

W. European ART motto: Culture and dialects. (Kassel 1982)
S. African ART Manifestation: Culture and RESISTANCE. (Botswana 1982)

ART MUST GET BEYOND AESTHETICS. AND Neurotics must get beyond psychoanalysis.

ART DANGERS. ONE'S ARTSTYLE CAN hinder changes in your lifestyle. I believe that the world also exist independent of my perception and conception of it. I would like everyone to remember that. Art can make one forget that. TOO much ABSTRACTION CAN DESTROY you.

but then * TOO many LOVES CAN confuse you
* too many tears can dissolve you.
* too much passion CAN MISguide you, too.

I avoid crimes of passion, or rather try to.

one does what one can

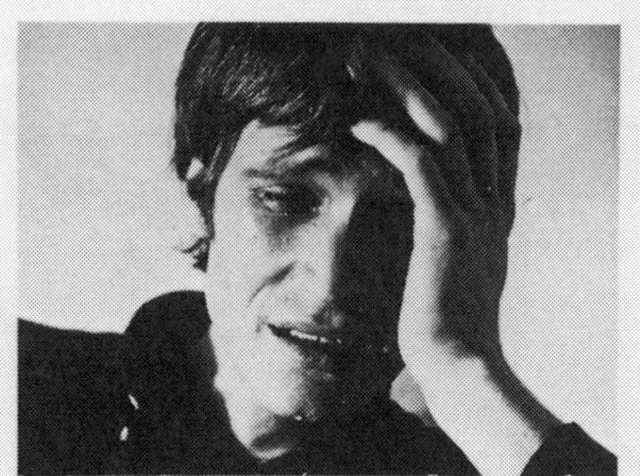

"I'm too sad to tell you". BAS JAN ADER.

Communication: Through ART we talk to strangers.

Even though a clear blueprint is missing - use the clue strips. private worlds show common problems. MAN AS biological being has remained essentially unchanged from the beginnings of civilization to the present.

Expressionism. To give up a style because you've outgrown it is as sad as leaving a loved one and as difficult. I don't want to worship my own handwriting. Expressionism usually deals with undefined feelings. I want to be a referential artist. Reference deals with that already named.* I want to transfere messages (readable feelings) e.g. emotions. Emotion is interpreted feeling. [* Names aren't always given/made by you though.] I am scared, because I don't know if ART will let it be used like that.

"MAN, man its a funny world he said we're got everything but we can't have it."
—(Bukowski)

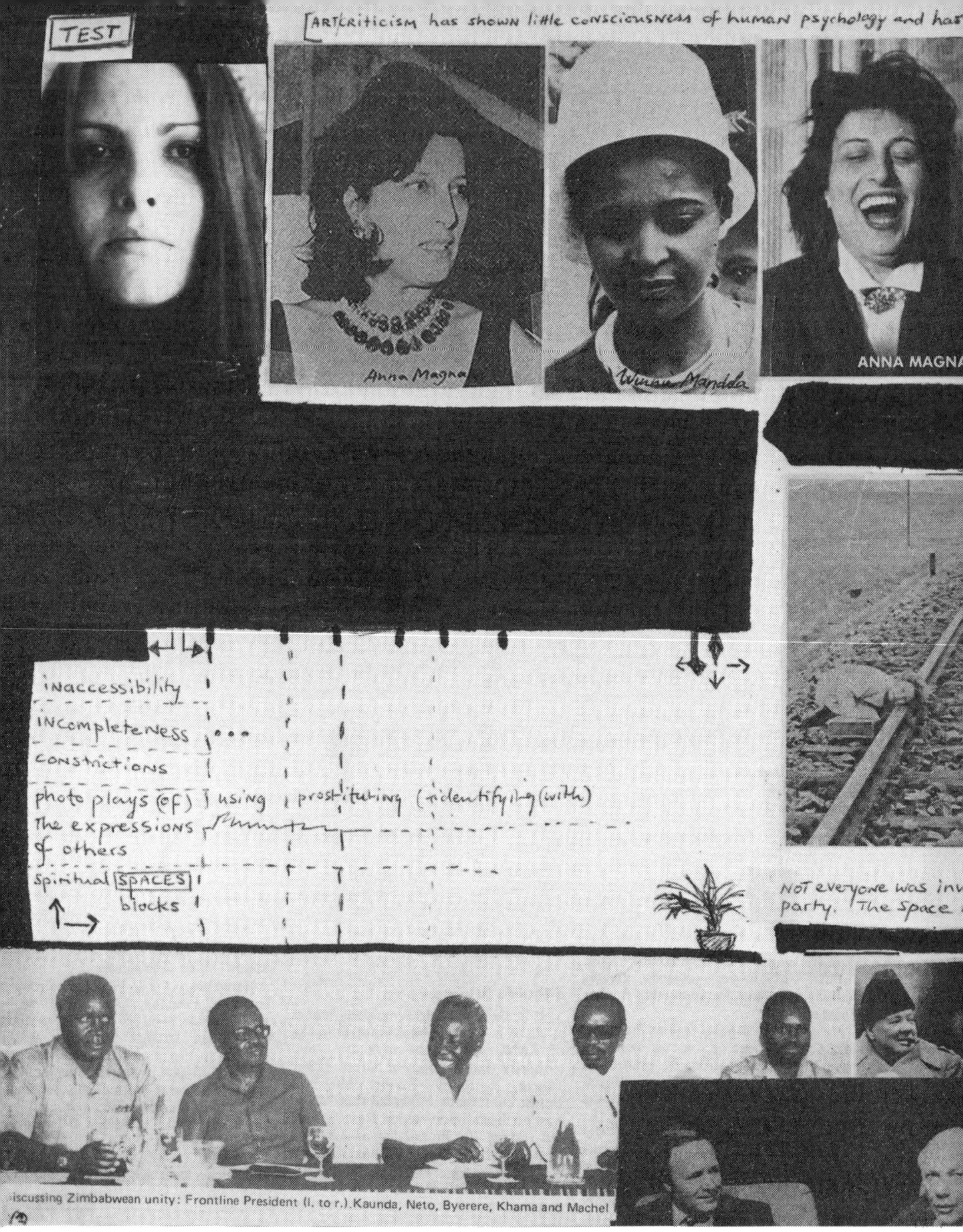

Discussing Zimbabwean unity: Frontline President (l. to r.).Kaunda, Neto, Byerere, Khama and Machel

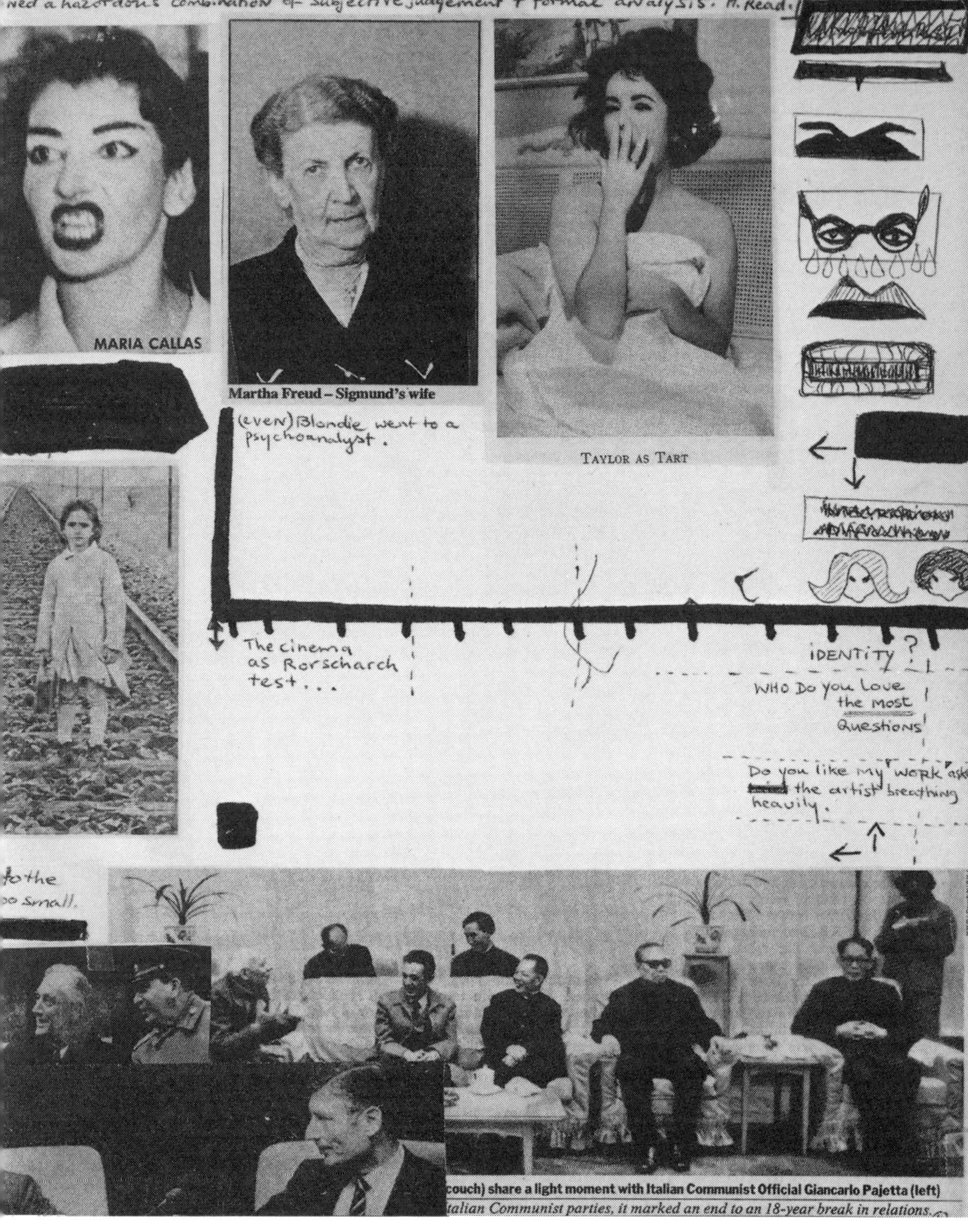
ned a hazardous combination of subjective judgement + formal analysis. H. Read
MARIA CALLAS
Martha Freud – Sigmund's wife
TAYLOR AS TART
(even) Blondie went to a psychoanalyst.
The cinema as Rorscharch test...
IDENTITY?
WHO Do you Love the MOST
Questions
Do you like my WORK asks the artist breathing heavily.
to the
oo small.
couch) share a light moment with Italian Communist Official Giancarlo Pajetta (left)
talian Communist parties, it marked an end to an 18-year break in relations.

PAIN GIVE it A NAME

Guilty of - Being at too big a distance from The concreteness of Life.

ABSTRACT: A designation applied to a partial aspect or quality considered in isolation, from a total object which is, in contrast, designated concrete.

ABSTRACTION.

ABSTRACTION: IN PSYCHOLOGY; The MENTAL operation by which we proceed from individual concepts to concepts of classes; from individual dogs to the notion of "the dog".

NARCISSISM. AS PSYCHIC DISTRESS: AN INABILITY TO FEEL or to become aroused. A persistent sense of illegitimacy which is at it strongest when one is being rewarded/ as being legitimate. A sense of being dead to the world.

APARTHEID

SEPERATION from.
TAKING apart. TEARING APART. KEEPING APART.

THE END "Neither a **life** perfected as art NOR AN **ART** perfected as life seems possible for us'

MARLENE AFTER SHE CRIED.

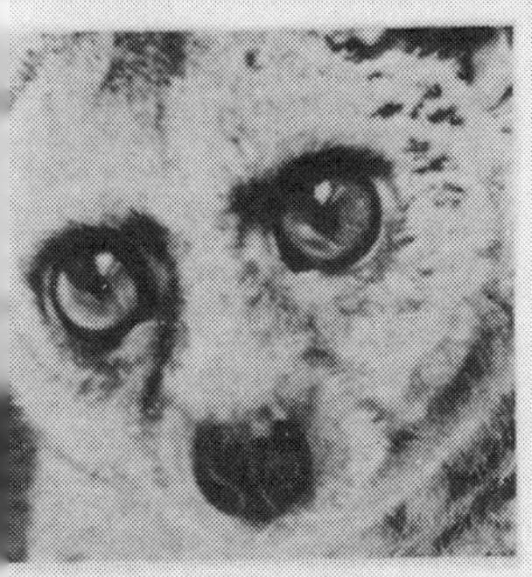

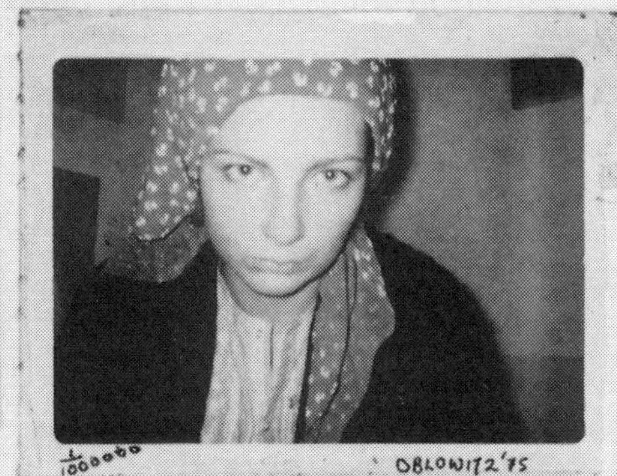

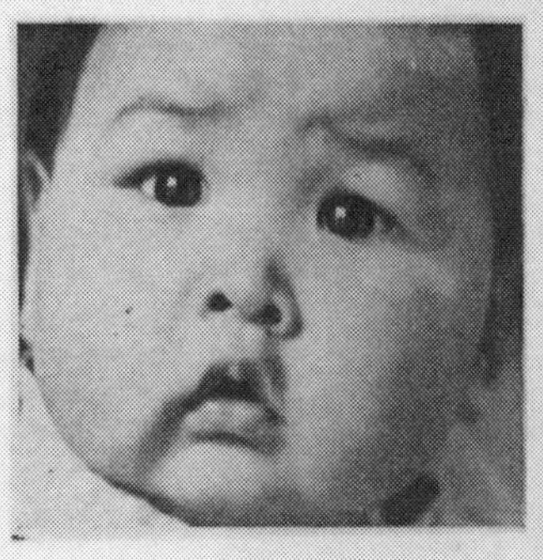

This is dedicated to those who 'grew up' in the 70's. Those who left and those who stayed . All those with the split hearts

Love Notes (The Lava-Edge)

I situate art not in reality

Back and forth
my heart is torn
between
different lonelinesses

I am the way towards death
with the breath of life on my tongue
while I leave you
your moist hand confuses you

Oh good God
I repeated
the whole
night through

Could you not come sooner
while it is still light
and the silence is clear and yellow
could you not come sooner
before the darkness blinds us

You don't need the keys
the door locks behind you
automatically

but in relation to desire

Death is natural
nothing
to be afraid of
but I'm going to
marry a pillow still
although
I've got enough
black velvet
to marry a king

We're running
out of nights
and they're bringing in
the artworks
for everyone to see

Sharpen your teeth my love
let my tongue move carefully between
till it reaches beyond your weeping
words

The moral of this story is that it's
almost impossible to distinguish
between an extinct volcano
and a dormant one

Unsatisfied Desire and the untrustworthy Language of Art

Some people die of their own passion.
Some by the passion of others.
And some simply die of illness
or another natural cause.
I am against it.

Art is not a mirror. Art is a translation
of that which you do not know, but of
which you want to convince others or
rather, that which no-one knows, but
by which everyone can be seduced into
believing that although 'it' is bad, 'it' is
good: it's good not to have what you
desire most.

I'll continue to cry for the doomed:
innocent brushstrokes, painterly
trances, the exotic other, 'love-fictions'.
To lipread and name the silence,
to use the dream that torture will stop
when the prisoner talks.

On Words and Images

I can see why many visual artists
dislike words in artworks. They feel
that words dirty the clear water that
has to reflect the sky. It disturbs
the pleasure of the silent image,
the freedom from history, the beauty
of nameless forms.

I want to name our pains.
I want to keep on changing
our names.

I know that neither images nor words,
can escape the drunkenness and
longing caused by the turning
of the world.
Words and images drink the
same wine.
There is no purity to protect.

The Eyes of the Night Creatures

My people were all shot
by a camera, framed,
before I painted them. They didn't know that I'd do this to
them. They didn't know by what names I'd call them.
They might even be disgusted by words like evil,
forgiveness, genes.
They weren't payed. They weren't directed.
They harbour (passive) tentions. Mental agression in a
passive body. No harm done. Death must be destroyed.
This is the Space Age. It is difficult to distinguish
between sadness and hatred.

Seemingly no-one believes in the capturing of 'souls'
anymore. (The Devil has become a type of playmate,
the product of a Playboy culture.)
The occult has become a tame game. Artworks are seen
and made as art. A structured language of fiction. These
attitudes ruling – my faces cannot be dangerous.
(I cannot be sued.)

I like putting myself down. It's a sort of arrogance.
Girls do that.
But BEWARE – I can see – you have long dark tunnels,
warm damp holes.
The truth can not be held as a cold bridge weapon,
to ward off pain.
I am not a cynic. I am touched by our bruiseability.
I laugh a lot.
My mouth is a small pink wound that needs airing.

My best works are erotic displays of mental confusions (with intrusions of irrelevant information)

A title determines the way one looks at the image. What is depicted is desire, what is central is deficiency. It all becomes more complex.
The aim of my work, I have come to believe, has always been to arouse in my audience (as well as myself) an experience of empathy with my subject matter (be it a scribble, a sentence, or a face) more so than sympathy. Sympathy suggests an agreement of temperament, and an emotional indentification with a person. Empathy doesn't necessarily demand that. The contemplation of the work (when it 'works') gives a physical sensation similar to that suggested by the work. I'm not a stylist, I'm a sensualist.

Notes

In Solitude
Art
that dull weed
engulfs my garden.

Why Women cannot keep it up with Art
Women are not
by their very nature
meant to suffer criticism.
This makes them so
wretched
that they cannot
keep it up.

Good Taste
Don't treat me like a child
you shrew
just because I'm short and fat
and dyed blond
by nature.
I'm (subtly)
fooling you.

Names of Things
I name these empty spaces
because of you.
I give them your name
without asking you.

At Night
Fast
flies
the night away
past
the speed of light.

Unconditional
Don't negotiate
with me
it's like the man said:
'Prisoners can't make
any appointments'.

Language Notes

Look –
my words
smell of ammonia and stain without
authority

Reject official sanctioned

LANGUAGE

write
Dutch
like Afrikaans

TALK

with bad accents
in distasteful
indelicacies
giggle
like young girls
pretend to be
dumb child
and
    wiggle
            your
                ass

The Plague Mentality

What are we going to do
now that we know
that the enemy is not outside the walls
but lives INTIMATELY within
and travels
in such ways
that EVERYONE and EVERYTHING
is suspect?

The Intuition of Danger

The artwork itself is not dangerous.
Murderous thoughts are not the same
as actually committing the murder.
I paint because I am scared.

Give me – artworks that vibrate
with a sense of their own futility.
Those committed by bloodhounds.
Smelling the stains even
in the whitest wash,
in the brightest rain!

Being aware of one's own bad breath.
The poisonous under-arm odours.
Delivering – thrilling reports on the
intoxication of fear and the acid
attraction of things you haven't said.

So – to quote the lady out of context –
'Because the danger remains the same
and the danger never seems to go away.'
I'll leave you in mid-air.
Without saying goodbye.

Fear of Babies

How do we dream
our dreams of peace
a race of small creatures
populating the areas of hatred
or the spheres of boredom

so

Share my bed
you sterilized lovers
and feel free
to do nothing
that would cause
the artist to give up
her aesthetic playthings
for the disorderly toys
of children

Pornographic Tendency

At the moment my art
is situated between
the pornographic tendency
to reveal everything
and the erotic inclination
to hide what it's all about

A Girl for all Seasons

Guilt

From these statements there's nothing you
can check and little you can predict.
Perhaps you're asking:
Who is responsible for these works?
You probably mean:
Whose fault are they?

Un-freedom

I've not come
to propagate freedom.
I've come to show the disease symptoms
of my time.
I'm a good example of everything
that's wrong with my time.

Reduction

Reduce – still, static, sober and systematic, they say,
the universal is not served
by references to the recognizable, the time-specific;
excess of necessity leads to ruin,
it's only the dumb
who don't wish to be released from this earth,
they say.

Distance

You – stranger – keep your distance.
I do not seek happiness in fulfilment,
but in the intensity of emotions.
And know that I can never love you
but will always avoid you
to spare you my eyes.

Titles

My works bear their names,
like one has to bear one's own history.
Drunk with associations and incest,
contaminated by all kind of illness and prejudices,
deliberatly wounded,
so that they will not become arrogant
and forget their very innards.

A-sexual

Where is the eroticism in the art of my generation?
My generation cherishes loneliness
prizing it even above sex.
They are so sensitive,
they are allergic to each other.

The Meaning of Drawing

Wir wollen uns lieben, aber wir wissen nicht wie Berlin graffiti

I make a distinction between drawings which I regard as autonomous works of art and drawings which are 'just drawings'. Not that the latter are necessarily inferior, but to me personally they are less fraught with meaning and hence more friendly.

These here are 'just drawings'.
Hand and head in relaxed partnership, susceptible to impressions received from working with the material (a well-tried method). In these drawings I have not used language (text) as a foreign or aggressive element (as I often do); the titles merely express the associative paths my thoughts take, together with the forms encountered on the way.

This kind of work keeps my circulation going in chilly spells. They are nonsensical works referring to a searcher for meaning.
Chilly spells are frequent.

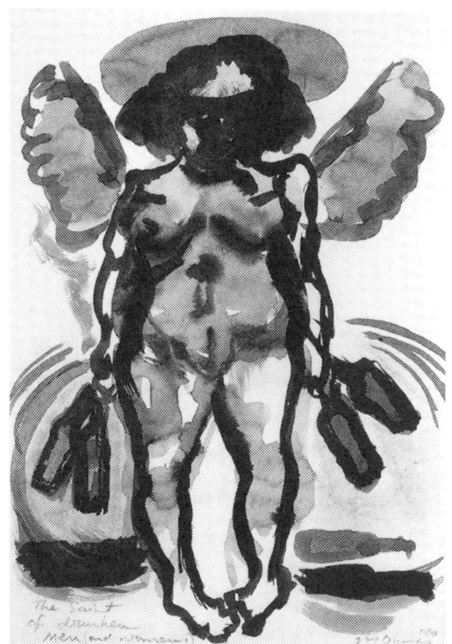

The Saint of drunken Men (and Women) 1990
29,7 x 21 cm

The surrealist tradition has become the basis of many drawings. Without the urge towards revolution and madness. Or should I say, drawings have become the cartoons of our small dreams.
Maybe drawing should never have become 'art' after all.
But just give them enough rope...

I am against
general ideas
the nude
the appropriation of images
the mystification of the untitled
the glorification of artistic doubt
the fuzzy edges of sensitivity
old sins
and useless guilt

Notes on the Private versus the Public

Notes on the Private versus	the Public
the individual vs	the group
the artist	the (his/her) public
the studio space	the gallery space
the working conditions	the exposition situations
the time of execution (maturation?)	the time of consumption (temporality)
the intimicy of the snapshot	the posed official photograph
the referential aspect of 'realist' figuration	the general appeal of abstraction (nonhistorical)
the specific	the universal
THE NAKED	THE NUDE
private problems	public media
private solutions	political disasters
the confession	the TV talkshow
	(the interview in a gossipcolumn or newspaper.)
the intentions of the artist	the 'explanations' of the critic (promotion or put down)
private embarassment	public jokes

Don't talk to strangers

the body as problem vs	the body as privilege
the male sex as opposition	the male sex as equal (equally vulnerable)

No more Interviews

1. I don't want to give any more 'spontaneous' interviews. It presupposes an ease which I don't have with my interviewer, or the interview situation. It's a sham spontaneity.
2. The informality of the spoken word and the formality of the written word are two separate things. Now more than ever.
3. A respect for, or making a distinction between, private and public matters is something that is being increasingly undervalued.
4. In oral conversations, gestures (along with tone, emphasis, allure) are extremely important. But the interviewer doesn't translate these things. I'm not there when he or she writes about me. And neither do I want him or her with me when I answer their questions. In this way there's no disguising the artificiality of the conversation, and the written material is more genuinely reflective.
5. I'm not an entertainer.
6. I can't think things over properly with a stranger facing me.
7. Art is not a suitable subject for snappy answers or the brilliant one-liner.
8. The opposite of openness is not always elitism. People have a fundamental need for privacy, particularly in a world bombarded with messages, and psychological snares and media manipulation, which have nothing to do with friendship or with in-depth research or analysis.
9. I don't speak Dutch.
10. I have a gallery that is aware of my points of view.

p.s. the title of my exhibition implies the extent of the problem.

No Smoking in public
Public secret. Public school = private school.

The intimate world of the child versus the public displays of interrogation, violence + law and order + security systems. The teachers teach politics. The teachers teach art, the laws of one's culture.

Human beings can't live without secrets.
That which is most important to one's well being is not public relations.

Selling one's Soul to the Devil

ART
like an occult science is
an ancient ritual as dangerous
as the first flare of attraction
between two people –
an unreliable situation
with unpredictable consequences.

Blind Spots

Painting and the problems of her bastard children

Are you also too incoherent to write a tightly structured piece? Do you think your own words sound far less important than those of others that have already been published? Do you also try to hide this inadequacy and inferiority complex under the (French) philosophical cloak of the text-that-writes-itself? I won't say that reality is just the same as TV-with-remote-control. A fragmented spectacle that matches my habit of never finishing my sentences. (Although that may well be the case.)

I'M IN FAVOUR OF IMPURE PAINTING

Please read (or reread) Theo van Doesburg (1919): 'Grondbegrippen der Beeldende Kunst' (Fundamental principles of visual art). He's extremely lucid about his basic principles. I like clarity: at least as far as it's possible to be clear in this tragic profession. It's quite unnecessary, especially these days, to pile on even more layers of ambiguity. We already know that, by definition, art can never be unambiguous. But that doesn't mean that we have to succumb to Duchamp's 'as stupid as a painter'. Gradually you'll realize I'm after something other than an exact artwork, although I can't (as yet) uphold my views with the same lucidity as he.

I went to art college in South Africa from 1972 until 1975. The painting teachers taught me that the 'illustrative' and the 'literal' were the greatest sins. As I understood it, the subject – whatever it might be – should not be clearly recognizable or, preferably, completely unrecognizable. Thus motifs derived from reality, the surface, the outward appearance of things, had to be reduced either by distortion or refinement. Imagination, not imitation. Who could disagree with that?

But I wasn't happy with the situation. Something was gnawing away at me. Pop music, literature and film used subjects that everyone could relate to, but which painting wasn't (any longer) permitted, able, or willing to tackle. Yet these were subjects that I was unwilling to accept as being, by definition, 'unpaintable'. Jeff Wall (Canada) talked about the concept 'The painting of modern life', (he himself makes Cibachromes, not paintings), which he considers the greatest task an artist can fulfil. He has a great respect for the painterly tradition, but doesn't rate the painting of today very highly. Perhaps you should read his book *Transparencies* (1986). His major contribution is that he questions the basic premises which underpin the concept 'depiction'. And he does it very well. I agree with him on many points. Nevertheless it's a great pity that it seems as if only 'media' artists have something meaningful to say about our cultural decline, or want to portray it. Generally speaking it's media-artists who still get all excited about notions like 'honesty', or about manifestations from the advertising world, or other power structures.

It strikes me that many art critics (and artists too) use the concept 'manipulation' as a compliment. Could this be because our pluriform and satiated society finds 'equating' less demanding than 'differentiating'? But Jeff Wall can't be accused of using words inaccurately. He demonstrates that a narrative motif doesn't necessarily have to produce an anecdotal image, or that socio-political interest doesn't perforce immediately lead to Agitprop, so long as there's enough visual intelligence present. But to return to my years at the academy and my attempts to become a modern artist who knows how to veil the origins of her work in such an ingenious way that all that remains are suggestions and vague suspicions extraneous to the work that no-one could possibly label as cheap. It's only too well-known that the use of sentimental, dramatic subjects can be a cheap way of attracting attention. And as a sensitive artist I, too, was particularly keen not to be cheap. Women in particular have to watch out not to be cheap. Easy effects can fade just as easily. Thus painting steers clear of readily recognizable images, leaving politics and eroticism to hetero and homo sex magazines, fashion magazines, World Press competitions, TV or the Third World. When, around 1870, Cézanne broke away from associatively charged themes, the benefit to art was enormous. But I can't evince the same respect for the many artists who still view the challenge of an exciting-picture-without-exciting-subject-matter as painting's sole task. (Although I have to admit that it can be pleasurable to leave the dirty work to 'others'.)

So under the heavy burden of Malevich, Mondriaan (and Marilyn Monroe), and in the knowledge that everything of value is invisible, and because of my love of Abstract Expressionism and everything that goes with it (particularly, therefore, Clement Greenberg), I felt a growing need to re-evaluate the concept 'realism'. Did it come from Andy Warhol who more or less said: 'It's all on the surface, not inside'? Even Beuys, who knew all there was to know about the connection between surface and depth, had sympathy for his so-called antithesis. Oh well… it's much too long a story...!

In conclusion I come to what I really wanted to talk about: Oliver Sachs's book *The Man who mistook his Wife for a Hat* (1985). The importance of this book becomes evident if we cease to experience subject-matter as a visual dead-end. The issue here, however, is not the difference between a word and an image. Even Magritte assumed that when he got up in the morning he was still partly Magritte. Identity is actually something other than having a specific name. (But they're often equated with each other figuratively speaking, as metaphor.) The central concern here is the recognition and evaluation of reality, which is essential to our survival as human beings. A sort of neurology of identity. The neurologist Dr. Sachs, (Einstein College, N.Y.), described the history of his patients' illnesses in narrative form. He's as concerned with the what as with the who. A return to the nineteenth century tradition where the central focus was the power of description. People need dramatic stories. The book deals with damage to the right half of the brain (called the primitive minor hemi-sphere), as opposed to the sophisticated left half (designed to deal with programming and schematization), which up to now has always formed the prime focus. For example: patient P suffers from a special form of visual agnosia (= inability to interpret stimuli to the sensory organs). On a visual level, P has lost all sense of the emotional, the concrete, the personal, and has had to fall back on the abstract and the categorical, like a computer. His illness began when he noticed that he (a music teacher by profession) was unable to recognize his students if they weren't speaking or moving, although, technically speaking, there was nothing wrong with his eyes. Also he mistook non-living objects for people. Dr. Sachs carried out perception tests on P which produced the following in relation to identification of reality:

1. Platonic solids – he had no problem with recognizing cubes and other abstract forms.
2. Playing cards – also no problem with stylized forms.
3. Cartoons – also no obstacle, because of the schematic nature of the data and the fact that determining characteristics could be isolated.
4. Television: a love scene between two people – he could neither identify facial expressions nor describe the situation.
5. Photographs of himself and family members: no recognition. Thus not a funny, but a tragic, situation.
6. A glove – he described it as a continuous surface, folded over, with five bulging pockets which could contain something. Although he had no idea what.

P was thus functioning as a machine. The world as representation no longer existed for him. He could no longer interpret or evaluate, all he was capable of were cognitive hypotheses, although there was nothing wrong with his intelligence or his powers of abstraction. A complete human being uses both hemispheres of the brain, but artists choose for themselves the areas they wish to focus on. I'm not trying to make an obtuse diversion, but rather to point-up that there are actual and important differences between the concepts 'representation' and 'abstraction', which is vital to recognize if people want to address them seriously. Read the book yourself and don't let yourself be clouded by loyalty to any art institution or advertising agency. It could be the beginning of something meaningful.

Warning

Love is not blind, no
The past will never die, no
Everything that glitters is blood

Naked Bodies

On the one hand – there is the immediacy of the senses...

I can recall with great accuracy how it physically felt
when, as a child, I unexpectedly stepped
with my bare feet on the slipperly snails
that appeared after the rains.

How I watched the frogs. Their heavy breathing,
their buldging eyes. The texture of their skin.

The moon disturbing the film-images
of the Drive-in theatre called the SKY VIEW.

How soft my grandmother felt to touch.
How blue she bruished. How the sun shone through
her almost transparent pink ears...

The painter kills
eats up the heart

But on the other hand – I know the endless sidesteps of the mind.

I've grown up with 'the politics of paradise'.
I know about the mingling of attraction and
disgust human beings feel when they look
at the skins of others. The thoughts they think.
The contradictions they dress up with careless 'intuition'.

And I am also aware of the differences between
human beings and artificial images. That oil and
paint, not flesh and blood, run through their veins.
My figures know that too. And like fallen angels do
they blame me (and you) for creating them
to exist in the land of abstraction – called art.

the living and in salt water

The Return of the Non-dead

Paintings tell stories
like zombies walk the earth.
I moved slowly from
the faces to the bodies.
From the eyes to the skin.
From the word to the flesh.

Snowwhite wants to compete
with the man of sorrows.
Snowwhite has to compete
with the man of sorrows.

Waiting Rooms (need TV)

Models wait
for artists to give them meaning.
Girls (use to) wait
for boys.
Patients wait
for doctors...

ART waits for no-one.
ART cares for no-one.
ART doesn't speak unless
it's spoken to.
ART is only metaphorically
a language, not literary.
ART does not follow the rules
of language.
The arbitrary and the particular
resist generalisations
necessary
for logical communication.
ART loves her enemies
more than her protectors.
ART loves to know. Everything.
ART has never been innocent.
ART has always been mediated.
Life has always been complicated.
All art eventually becomes ART,
and solves nothing.

The Question of Human Pink

Colour

I don't know much about colour really
I use it intuitively.

I don't know much about racism really
my knowledge is skindeep.

What do you mean, he said.
Oh, she said, didn't you know
all scars have a pink that shows.

The Exotic versus the Neurotic

The Dutch, among others, pay
hommage they say
by buying African art, by trying to paint
like them.
I cannot do that
I pay in other ways.

All the white artists want to be black.
I can't pretend I'm not
stuck with snowwhite
as my name.

Sexual Organs

Between the motif and the traces
of the hand
falls the shadow.

Birth

To create an artwork
(to make an image of)
and to give birth
(to an other human being)
have essentially nothing to do
with one another.
Yet this is no reason to stop loving
metaphors or avoiding the unrelated.
But the poetry that results from mixing
different kinds of language,
dissappears into sloppy thinking,
when we imagine that these
differences can ever be solved
harmoniously; or even worse, when
we forget that these realities we are
mixing, show a beautiful and often
cruel indifference towards each other.

~~Humanist Figurative Paintings~~ PAINTINGS of the

thinking about —

humanist

characterized by Men-"as"-

The Americans

Pollock – the heart
~~Salle~~ – the chill
Warhol – the social realist → Disaster
Fishl – the sexual guilt
Golub – the political guilt.

Alice Neel – beautiful portrait of andy Warhol

her people is not trying to be a-historical beings + not universal signs. They're clothes are of the fashion of the day — and yet the paintings are not dated.

Alex Katz – the flatness of modernism combined with recognizable imagery.
Life at it's better (?) moments.

The 70's
Richard avedon portraits of his father
Diane Arbus.

Longo – "I think of myself as a non-figurative painter. using figures. I don't actually give a fuck about figures."

Men in the cities

Philiph Guston – the only artist who could paint the feel of a hangover.

Frida Kahlo's still lives.

short affairs
Fr. Bacon's men — too controlled / mannerist
De Kooning's women — too elegant
Clemente's fingers in holes — too sweet

David's → Death of Marat
munch →
Holbein — the
I used his "dead christ"'s co
for my "pa
of nati

Nolde —
I used his
as inspi
my "s

Rembr

Verme

Soutine's distortions —

the

Beuy

Che Guevara
the Art is the

(Lupertz
Reco

~~...~~
...MAN FIGURE

...gurative painting in Europe since world WAR II has been
...sters, I try to get away from it, but it's very difficult

The flemish primitives.
The sexuality of Christ
paintings of the dead

HODLER's drawings of his wife dying
Monet's – wife on her death bed.
Stephen McKenna – "Dead nude"
picking up the imagery from the 19th C that stopped with the 20th C emphasis on abstract art.
Not regression, but re-interpreting.

Representation + the crisis of INTERPRETATION.
Terry Atkinson – (Political Bodies)

Manet – The master of the unrelated figure

(Degas bathroom)

Rainer

Seurat – favorite drawings (black + white) of a leg.

Early Baselitz. – Dismembered males.
My favorite painting of a foot

...ity
...inism
...arity
...esis
..."glow"
...ours of
...dele"
...ers around
...or for.
...age
...t – the warmth of the flesh
... – the dignified distance
...lt –
...w.
...fraid
... storm.
...et – heaviness
...eight of the flesh
...m trend's "the ordinary"
...ERMANS
A big man
draws tender +
...rait drawings
the female body
...d her functions.
...no manneristic horror.
...mmendorf don't paint people
...ould get depersonalized figures → as most figurative art do these days

The Origin of the Species

A child is born on a certain day
but the birth of an artwork
is impossible to calculate
and it's origin is impossible to find.

The beginning (or the end)
of a story is suggested
but no tales are told.
Accidents happen.

The relationships between the
artworks show 'missing links'
which are most severe between
closely allied works and varieties.

My memory disfigures my feeling.
My imagination disfigures
my memory.
My sources vary.

I paint after the photo –
the distorted afterglow
of chemical reproduction,
filtered through my clumsy attempts
towards natural perception,
and the preservation
of a dubious habit.

Couples

I am the third person
observing the bad marriage
between art and life
watching the pose and the slip
seeing the end in the beginning.

Die meisie met die spraakgebrek
says yes but means no.

The World is flat

The question was: Why do painters still paint?
For me the reason is clear. Because the world is flat. This obvious, though serious fact is not yet common knowledge, but will become clearer as we approach the end of the 20th century. One should however not answer questions about art without evaluating the keywords, and recognizing the assumptions that are implicit in the language used by those who try so hard to push, praise and publish about art. The terms by which the artists are questioned frame the works. It is peculiar that with this supposed variety around (all this difference) in the artworld, when we read about it, it is all described in the same way.

Either we're all doing the same thing, or we're all writing the wrong things. I fear the last is more true than the first. A good artist struggles with the specific. A good text should strive for similar fine distinctions and avoid broad generalizations.
Some examples:

Photography
It is not the relationship between painting and photography that is the most prominent question today. The fact is that the photographic, not photography as a specific medium but a particular mode of signifying, is affecting all the arts at the moment.

Meaning
This term is experiencing an extreme identity crisis. After being out of circulation for a while, or mentioned primarily in a negative sense (because of its literariness), it is now thoughtlessly being overused. Everything and anything that is called meaningfull is supposedly better than that which is meaningless. Yet that is not necessarily so.

Broodthaers said about his work: 'It was an attempt to deny, as far as possible, meaning to the word, as well as the image.'
General Idea said of their Miss General Idea Beauty pageant: 'Glamorous objects open themselves like whores to meaning, answering need with vacancy, wanting to be penetrated by the act of recognition.'[1] This 'act of recognition' brings me to the other Big Misunderstanding.

Representation
I quote from the magazine *De Rijksacademie* 'Formalism on the one hand and theatricality on the other can be seen as two extremes of a complementary duo in art: form and representation or form and content.'

This is absolutely not true. One cannot equate representation with content, this is a very popular misconception. Painting (especially) is not a registration of facts or a documentation of information. It is an interpretation. It is forced to be so by its nature.

One's 'object matter' is never strictly speaking one's subject matter.

Sherrie Levine and Louise Lawler offer a critique of representation as traditionally defined. They collaborated under the collective title *A picture is no substitute for anything.* This brings us to the core of the matter.

Content

What do we mean when we talk about the content of a work of art? Content is not one thing. Content is a complex network of relationships. The best art essay I've read so far is that by Thomas McEvilley.[2] He focusses out attention on the following thirteen categories.

Thirteen Ways of Looking at a Blackbird

1. Content that arises from the aspect of the artwork that is understood as representational.
2. Content arising from verbal supplements supplied by the artist.
3. Content arising from the genre or medium of the artwork.
4. Content arising from the material of which the artwork is made.
5. Content arising from the scale of the artwork.
6. Content arising from the temporal duration of the artwork.
7. Content arising from the context of the work.
8. Content arising from the work's relationship with art history.
9. Content that accrues to the work as it progressively reveals its destiny through persisting in time.
10. Content arising from participation in a specific iconographic tradition.
11. Content arising directly from the formal properties of the work.
12. Content arising from attitudal gestures (wit, irony, parody and so on) that may appear as qualifiers of any of the categories already mentioned.
13. Content rooted in biological or physical responses, or in cognitive awareness of them.

He acknowledges that certain artworks can deny or contradict some of these categories and that the list of contents that arises among the categories could be extended indefinitely.

1 From *Revelations from the Doghouse 1968–1984*, General Idea

2 From 'On the manner of addressing clouds', *Artforum*, Summer 1984, p. 61– —70

Terminologies

Terminologies have become warped.
The word intuition and other mystifying terms are often bandied about indiscriminately by artists. But I believe in the magic of words and, therefore, think people should use them with care. We've lost credibility because we no longer do what we claim to be doing. We're 'pepping up' our profession with terminology culled from other, more dangerous, fields. It's not just a matter of the sort of terms applied to us, but, more particularly, of the terms used by artists themselves.
We're often extremely sloppy in our use of analogies. People writing about Rob Scholte's work in the Netherlands usually focus on the fact that he appropriates the images of others. But reproduced images are public property. They belong to everyone. To me, there's nothing essentially inappropriate, warped, about that. But what I do find questionable is the appropriation of terms from outside art which are primarily intended to elevate the status of art: war and religious terminologies, for example. We want to make use of the exotic in religion (of real religion) without being willing to pay the price.

Whether we wish to recognize it or not, making art removes us from life as a dynamic process. That's why I find statements like 'life is art' completely meaningless – too over-simplified, a blanket term. Equating the terms 'art' and 'creativity' is a clumsy parallel. I'd like to quote Frans Kellendonk. (In 1986 he gave a lecture entitled 'Idolen' [Idols], as part of the series 'De Brandende Kwestie'.) He argued against realism and in addressing the premise that art is supposed to represent a need for solace, he said:

'Art which seeks to equate itself with life, or to harness the form of images which function outside the safe framework of art, loses out, in most cases, to 'real' propaganda which generates its own tension.'

Kellendonk makes a distinction between aesthetic emotion and ordinary, every-day emotions. He said he could cope with seeing blood in every-day life but not on film or television.

'It's fairly obvious and yet it's still generally believed that unreal situations created by art conjure up real emotions in the art-lover, and that artistically minded people are also automatically civilized people. But art-emotions are ontologically different from every-day emotions and, before there can be any discussion about the moral effect of art, psychology must first establish the precise status of art-emotions.'

Death as Model

Back to a dark source of inspiration. And this brings us to sentiments such as pain and sorrow, which now – in our own time – are bound up with kitsch.
I'm interested in artists who take death as a model. So often Andy Warhol is only seen in relation to money. But for me, he's one of the few artists whose art addresses death and the sentiments of our time without succumbing to sugary or over-dramatic imagery. A good synthesis between realism and artificiality.

I like art that wrestles with the eternally unequal relation between its sources of life and its artificial nature. Art which draws on corporality, while always acknow-ledging that, in the final analysis, it remains unnatural.

Why is there so little that moves you? Because we want to ignore evil and deny the body.
Being touched has not so much to do with succeeding. The problem with contemporary art is that it's far too selfconscious. To my mind, when art is too well-orchestrated, when it knows only too well how to manipulate its public and knows exactly what the public wants, then inevitably emotion is absent because, in my opinion, art that moves you has something ungainly about it, is in some way bound up with a combination of hesitation and something going wrong.
If art is too shielded and protected we end by smothering it to death. Mishima: 'If art is not constantly threatened and stimulated by things outside its domain, it exhausts itself.'
He said that everyday on getting up you must practise dying and imagine all kinds of ways in which you might die. But you must make sure that you've got your make-up at hand, because you must look good on the day of your death.

The Artwork as Misunderstanding

There is a crisis with regard to Representation.
They are looking for Meaning as if it was a thing.
As if it was a girl, required to take her panties off
as if she would want to do so, as soon as
the true interpreter comes along.
As if there was something to take off.

Miss Interpreted

What is the matter, little Miss Muffet?
Why so upset; because a spider
sat down beside her?

This is a question I can ask myself.
Did I not invite this misadventure
into my parlour? Sleeping with my door
open at night, smiling at perfect strangers?
This is reminiscent of the controversy surrounding
Rape, where the line between
seduction and whatever-it-was-you-got is a crucial point.

At the beginning of the 90's, or the end of the 20th century, it is evident that the workings of suggestive artworks need re-examination. It has become clear that all artworks that SUGGEST narrative put the viewer on trial. Or 'on stage', if you prefer the terminology of the theatre to that of the courtroom. In literature, in theatre, think of Ionesco, Beckett, Genet..., and in film: Resnais, Godard..., this is old news (in certain recent advertising there is an analogous development). They have dealt with ambiguous images in works that are built to accomodate a multiplicity of equally plausible interpretations. Yet works that do give the outsider the feeling of: If-you-don't-know-it's-no-use-me-telling-you. Wasn't that what Gary Cooper said to Grace Kelly in High Noon? Yet all of these media deal with a type of storytelling and an unfolding of time from the start. While painting is ontologically of a different order and by its character 'out' of time. So even when you deal with paintings that show affinities with these artforms, you cannot ignore these important differences. While 20th century's art in general 'expresses' rather tan 'explains' and 'veils' rather than 'exposes', 'The privileging of reading over "imagening" was of central significance for conceptual art. (Linguistic Theory have taught us to read pictures, rather than to imagine meaning.)'[1]
So here we are bending ourselves over backwards to 'read out' and 'read in'. Fools rushing in where angels fear to tread, eager to enter the work and posses the secret.

An old love of mine once said,
just give me the one thing
I know you can't give me,
give me a simple yes or no.

I never liked either of these terms
and if you're not prepared for a
never-ending answer, don't ask me no questions,
I'm not deliberately hiding something.
Take your healing hands off my broken sentences.

Night time

Night in the city is a fabricated thing where the stars are invisible. I like filmstars. Movies are shown in the dark. I like sitting in the dark especially during the day. Paintings are made in the dark.

Larger than life

I don't have any conception of how big an average head is. (I don't really have a conception of how big anything is, for that matter!) I've never been interested in anatomy. In that respect I relate like children do. What is experienced as the most important, is seen as the biggest, irrespective of actual or factual size.
In movies everything is larger than life and yet you experience that as real(istic), all my faces are much bigger than human scale, yet no-one seems to acknowledge that, not that that is so surprising seeing that this capacity for enlargement is one of the principle characteristics of photographic vision and a method used by many an artist of our day. (Compared to artists like Chuck Close and Alex Katz my jumps in scale are relative.) From blowing up to zooming in, for me the 'close-up' was a way of getting rid of irrelevant background information and by making the facial elements so big, it increased the sense of abstraction concerning the picture plane. The use of photographic projection eliminated the main compositional and proportional choices. The elimination of the background also did away with the place of being, and environmental context.

Isolation

As the isolation of a recognizable figure increases and the narrative character decreases (contrary to what one might initially assume that this lack of illustrative information would bring about), the interpretative affects are inflamed. The titles redirect the work; however do not eradicate the inherent ambiguity. One cannot interpret the painting of *Jule – die vrou* without entangling some of the root metaphores applied not only to the female, but to the idea of portrayal in general.

My Night Creatures are alone. But if you compare them to the metaphysical loneliness and alienation that Giacometti conveys, they strike a warm pop(ular) note, or compared to the chill of Longo's *Men in the Cities* or Barbara Kruger's aggressive tones, I look like Dolly Parton.

Close ups

In an essay on Luchino Visconti: *l'Innocente*[2] (1976), Willem Jan Otten writes about the method of the zoom. 'It is the movement of the lens that can bring a picture closer, WITHOUT HAVING TO MOVE THE CAMERA FROM ITS PLACE.' He makes a distinction I have never thought of before, but which relates to the close-ups of my Night Creatures. It is not so much that you go to the object, (or subject for the matter) but that it is drawn towards you and sucked out of the environment (or context) until it becomes a close-up. It is a powerful and tiranical method, for one thing, the human eye has no zoom lens. For the mediocre filmer it means instant failure.
When he describes the end of the movie he mentions that Visconti avoids a Wagnerism (which is not unknown to him) 'He is using the zoom much less and at the eventual suicide scene the camera stays at a large distance. As a camera should when someone comes to their end.'
I have used the close-up only for the human face. This method achieves an intimidating and confrontational effect which was what I wanted. Images combining intimacy (or the illusion of that) with discomfort. Eyes, no matter where the gaze is directed, have strong impact. It is selfevident that the quick cheap thrills of immediate psychological impact can also turn out to be very tedious.

Couples

I did not paint Freud, instead I painted his wife.
'Western Thought has always worked by oppositions. The law organizes the thinkable through oppositions. (Whether as irreconcilable dualities, or in comparative uplifting dialectics.) We think in couples even when we try very hard not to – based on the force of the copula, of copulation'.[3]
Now I'm thinking of William Wegman and his dog Man Ray. His work can make me actually laugh about these matters. How he plays with the awareness of how we try to domesticate the other. And then there is Bluebeard and his last wife. They turned into one another like Bergman's *Persona*.

Painting a naked man

I have drawn many things, but I have not made a painting of a naked man more than once, well, twice, the first embarrassed attempt was in 1975. The title of the painting done in 1987 is *The Particularity of Nakedness*. The title was inspired by the re-reading of John Berger's *Ways of Seeing* (1972), in which he draws a distinction between the 'nude' and the 'naked' in European oilpainting. At artschool in the 70's it was clear that no-one was inspired by the nude drawing classes anymore. The women (of colour) who posed at the university had been there for many many years. Being a model had become their occupation. They had posed themselves into (still-life-like) generalised objects, devoid of erotic (or any kind of) energy. The rare occasions that the male nude (white) was aquired, it led to giggles or indifference but not to concentration. Now it seems that it was not the nude I was looking for, nor the posing figure, but the erotic conditions of life that I was after. Two 'subjects' confronting each other.

'Apart from the necessity of transcending the single instant and of admitting subjectivity, there is, as we have seen, one further element which is essential for any great sexual image of the naked. This is the element of banality, which must be undisguised but not chilling. It is this which distinguishes between voyeur and lover. Here such banality is to be found in Rubens's compulsive painting of the fat softness of Hélène Fourment's flesh which continually breaks every convention of form and (to him) continually offers the promise of her extraordinary particularity'.[4]

As we move from the *Specific* to the *Type* we come to:

Voyeurism

Why do my pictures escape the 'voyeuristic gaze'. This was a question put to me recently. My reaction was: I'm not a Peeping Tom, I'm a painter, I'm not even a photographer. But I think the answer is in the J. Berger quote above. The aim is to 'reveal', not to 'display'. It is the discours of the Lover. I am intimately involved with my subject matter in this painting. I am not disengaged from the subject of my gaze. With photographic activities it is possible that they who take the picture leave no traces of their presence, and are absent from the pictures. Paintings exist as the traces of their makers and by the grace of these traces. You can't TAKE a painting – you MAKE a painting.

Private parts

Some comments from my viewers on the painting *The Particularity of Nakedness*: A woman (writer) told me she was very disappointed in seeing this work, she used to enjoy my older, more conceptional work, so much but what was I doing now – painting pictures for gay men. She called it a homosexual painting?! She said my male

was too passive. Will we ever get beyond the hetero/homo dualism? A man (museum director) told me that the painting was a failure due to too many horizontals. It was apparently very hard to paint a good painting without any vertical elements. Just recently I saw that John Baldessari did a work *Horizontal men* (1984). He said it was the obverse of a man vertical, the measure of things. It was a vulnerable alternative. I liked that.
The difficulties with this work made me think of the depictions of the sexual organs of Christ (remember *The Sexuality of Christ?*[5]) although somehow in the reverse. My male image was experienced as 'not strong enough'. Both parties wanted him erected one way or another.

Footnote
If we return to the female nude and notions of ideal beauty, we come to Manet who broke the rules with his *Olympia*, but then we see idealism replaced by the 'realism' of the prostitute, '(...) who became the quintessential woman of early avant-garde twentieth century painting'. John Berger does not make the link, but I do see a relationship between the position of the homosexual and the image of the prostitute in our western culture. The male equivalent of the 'bad woman' (the prostitute) is the gay male.

Distortion
The human Tripod is not really a man. He is a construct. It is a painting relating the world of drawing with the world of photography. This reminds me of Jeff Wall's *No* (1983). There you see a 'one-legged' man walking passed a woman in the street. The man is 'distorted' through photography. You don't notice it unless pointed out to you because you know that although you don't see the other leg, you do see the shadow. So you don't miss it.
A Picasso painting (more drawing than painting) of a boy in clownsuit with three legs is an attempt at deciding where to put the leg. It's a formal consideration. We don't read any other significance into the fact that his painting did not cover up the signs of his drawing, structuring or composing the work. This was still in his blue (or pink) period. It is because we know the history of his art. He is dead now and can thus also be looked at from the end to the beginning. (The Greeks entered death backwards in order to keep their past before them.)
John Baldessari used a photograph of a man that actually had only one leg, and gave him 'back' his missing leg through photographic intervention, art as an act of healing he described it. For me art is more a cleaning up process. I keep everything as valuable that presents itself to me and then I don't know how to get rid of it again. I don't live with my paintings. It is a relief when they go away. I don't enjoy looking at my own work.

My paintings are not the executions of ONE idea or emotion that goes from (a) intention to (b) artwork. (Our notions of cause and effect are also in bad shape.) Drawings are closer and quicker in conveying immediate feelings. The more you move towards paintings the darker the wood becomes through which Little Red Riding Hood goes and it's not only the wolf, but also the wicked witch and the seven dwarfs and Judas and Jesus and the journalists, that she has to face.

Humour
Once something has been made to look ridiculous, it can never carry the same authority again.

Motherhood
Now I'm not one of the boys anymore.

Motives
I was accused by women of misusing babies. It has been said that I mistreat grown-ups, but at least they could defend themselves and babies couldn't. And even if a baby looked like that, they did not want to see them in that way, it was said. Then I was accused of speaking the truth but apologizing for it. Then I was very tired.

Keep out of reach of children
Art is not meant for children
Like poison and medicine
it should be kept out of reach

Drama
The playwrite Arthur Adamov recorded how an ordinary street incident first made him aware of the dramatic possibilities of mutual solitude. He saw one day two young girls passing a blind beggar on the street. As they passed arm-in-arm, oblivious of the beggar, they sang a popular song of the day. 'J'ai fermé les yeux, c' était merveilleux' (I closed my eyes, it was wonderful). It's exactly the opposite of what has always been thought dramatic. Here we have the abscence of communication, the abscence of human sympathy and emotion and above all, the abscence of conflict.[6]

When I think of Rembrandt and dramatic moments I think of *The offering of Isaac* where the gesture of the hand pushing on the boy's face is unforgettable, or *Lucretia* with the dagger. With my own paintings, apart from a wine glass or two, or some camera's, the characters are mostly inactive and empty handed. In most cases the drama is psychological rather than pictorial (especially in the portraits). As the potential for narrative increases by including attributes and/or action (the small boy in *Snowwhite and the Wrong Story*; the clutching of the camera in *Snowwhite and the Broken Arm...*) the paintings become more dramatic in a theatrical sense. In the *Black Drawings*, however, we are 'back' where we started with the Night Creatures, in some essential way. The narrative has desolved into 'presence'. The viewers are back in the courtroom.

1 Nicolas de Ville on Gerard Hemsworth, in: *Between Shopping and Reification, Self Portraits*, cat. Matt's Galerie, London, 1978
2 l'Innocente, 1976
3 Alice Jardins, *Death Sentences: writing couples and ideology*, 1983
4 John Berger in *Ways of Seeing*, 1972
5 Leo Steinberg, *The Sexuality of Christ in Renaissance Art and in Oblivion*, 1983
6 *The Theatre of Protestand Paradox*, G.E. Wallworth N.V., New York, 1971

Ask me no questions and I'll tell you no lies

Intentions unclear (or never trust an artist).
How do you know my love is true?
How do you know I'm not a fake?
Why do you insist on my authenticity
when I warn you against my non-integrity?
Art is a low risk, high-reward crime.

My Brain

My brain, my bank, my archive, my copies,
my country is a small room filled with other people's traces.

My brain is a compost heap.
My art a compound expression.

As a magpie collects everything that glitters
as a dung beetle collects everything that stinks
so my savage joys are brought about.

Give the People what they want

In this world there are only two tragedies: one is getting what one wants, the other is not getting what one wants. Oscar Wilde

What is the work about?
Is it about eroticism?
No it's not tender enough, he said.
Is it about cruelty?
Is it that nasty?, I asked.
He said – it's sardonic.
Well, I said – isn't that the spirit of Africa?
No, he said – that's not Africa, it's you.

Bad Girls

People always want to know what my real hair colour is, as if that would reveal something essential.

Rosemarie Trockel is not whorish, neither is Cindy Sherman, nor Jenny Holzer ('Protect me from what I want') and certainly not Barbara Kruger. Neither in their capacity as artists nor in their outward appearances. (And they're not painters either.) Currently there's a new generation of female artists who cultivate a kind of 'bad girl' reputation. (They're mostly not painters either.) Barbara Bloom and I – the city girl and the country girl – once asked ourselves whether, in terms of art, we should be primarily the good bad girl or the bad good girl? I'm too detached to be really bad.

A Cheap girl

The Fine Arts are not sexy. They're too smart (arsed) and too extravagant(lasting)ly tasteful.

I'd love to make paintings that have the same kind of sex appeal as soul music. Aretha Franklin with R.E.S.P.E.C.T., Otis Redding with The Midnight Hour – my favourite LP ever... Janis Joplin – Cheap Thrills!

It was a compliment when someone once described my work as Cheap Thrills.
It wasn't meant as a compliment.

Popularity

The popular imbues each era with its own morbid symptoms and front-page photos. I like popular things. My chief sources are public images (intermingled with private snapshots and statements by others). What could be more inspiring and irritating than the images of dead, or almost unrecognizably mutilated concepts (once so dearly cherished) on the battle field of Art? Only the Babel in one's own head. You never make it in the media that way (Andy Warhol excepted).
Whatever, I'm not a real Pop artist. Maybe there was too much pathos in 'Action Painting', but in 'Pop Art' there wasn't enough Blues (Warhol excepted).

Half-heartedness

Yes, I'm half-hearted and cowardly. A split heart rather than a split personality! Art is heart-rendingly hard and unnaturally soft. I wasn't brought up with it and doubt its power. I want you to love me. I'll give you everything, you can take my name, only you can't have my heart. Art is an inscrutable, many-handed monster. I know it doesn't care about me.

I might just as well eat my words.

Sex and violence

It has been said that addressing or depicting subjects like sex and violence is the easiest way to attract attention. This is hard to deny but, as far as painting is concerned, it's not entirely true. For a long time, trend-setting painters thought that the most respectful and intelligent way of dealing with this, was simply to ignore it. When I was young I thought that only an elderly Englishman still did it. The few socio-politically conscious visual artists that still did it were not painters. But painting didn't renounce its relationship with the erotic entirely, by defining itself as a primarily physical, sensual surface. But sex and violence hit it off much better in the photographic field (and film in particular). Prolonging the suspense fuels the excitement. I wrote in 1988: 'The painter kills the living and eats up the heart in salt water', but I don't know what happens afterwards when the breath dissolves in paint. The longer I'm involved in painting, the stupider I become.

Liberty, Equality and Fraternity

Chris Dercon wrote in 'Am I now getting sentimental':'True images serve to remind us that we are not alone in the world.'[1] A wonderful sentiment, but not one that I can endorse because that's not how I experience it. Talking about the appreciation of artworks, Pasolini once said that it's when one feels free enough to enjoy the freedom of others. Quite a statement. For me, this emphasis on freedom doesn't represent our communality but our aloneness. This aloneness is not necessarily sickly. Nor does it have to be tragic. The most attractive thing about others, for me, is their otherness.

And then I'm not talking about exotica but erotica. The intimacy necessary to make that experience possible inevitably excludes me from group events. Liberty, Equality and Fraternity don't really like one another at all.

Religion

With voodoo or other religious rituals, the body is instinctively afraid to surrender to the Great Forces, because one experiences symptoms similar to those felt at the onset of death. Your brothers and sisters in faith may dance together, but YOU have to learn to let go of the body yourself. A process which holds out no sympathy from or for others. It's not that I want to elevate the creation, or evaluation, of art to these heights. On the subject of art Duchamp rightly said: 'As a religion it's not as good as God.'

Politics

1994 will see the first ever introduction of the democratic vote for all people in South Africa. I wouldn't mount this show with this title there now. And as Spike Lee would say: if you don't understand why not, you're probably white.

Playing for time

I was asked to write something about this exhibition, but actually I'm still tongue-tied. One of the good things about art is that people can state something themselves, without having been asked or the feeling that someone's expecting it. A childish, neurotic feeling steals over me as soon as someone asks or invites me to do something. Everything that is false or contrary in me rises up. As the interest in the work increases, so do the questions. The less that is asked of me, the haughtier my silence. But once given the right to speak, I begin to blush.

Postscript

It has been said: men make history, women autobiographies.

I'm aware that I've used a great deal of sexual terminology, but it's all bound up with my subject-matter.

No, they're not all self-portraits.
No, it's not always my daughter. No, I had a happy childhood.
No, I've never been in therapy.
No, I've never slept with museum directors.
Yes, I find compassion the most difficult thing there is and
not compatible with creativity.
Yes, I find myself the best example of evil.

1 *Parkett*, no.33, 1992

Female

1. The background of my drawings and the importance in regard to previous work.
When I was 12 years old, I thought, the only Big problem in life was Death.
Then I discovered Racism.
In 1991–1992 I made a group of 112 drawings called *Black Drawings*. Among other things, it was an attempt to exhibit my own unease, fear and admiration for the individuals grouped together under the term called 'Black'. In artistic terms (the suddenly very popular) area of 'the other' comes to mind. We(?) have to come to terms with 'them'(?).

Then I turned 21 years old and discovered Sexism.
Obtaining the anti-conception pill was the first act I did that celebrated my entree into adulthood. The first signature I put without asking my mother's permission or approval. (I knew she would not approve.) Without the discovery of the pill, I would probably not even be an artist today.

In 1992–1993 I made this group of many drawings, called *Female*. These faces have no background. They are placeless. We do not know, they do not show, where they came from and where they are going to. Like illegal aliens, they know, that those who attract too much attention, play and could pay with their lives. And when their time runs out, these watery images will wash away like 'tears in the rain'.[1]

2. The relation to the 21st Century – our future.
'We' already went to 'them'.
Now 'they' are coming to 'us'.

3. Artistic research, methods, cosmology.
The best thing Picasso (the replica of God) said: 'I don't search, I find', that's what God said when He placed His cross on the earth and founded the world. That's what I say when I see newspapers and images made by others.

1 Rutger Hauer in the movie *Blade Runner*

Drawings and the People who look at them

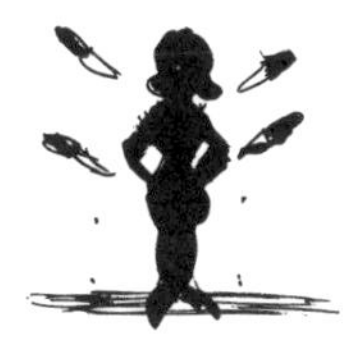

Three Blind Mice
throwing the dice.
Playing it safe
in the places between art and life.
Closing my eyes when they
throw the knife.

When I paint, I try not to be silly,
but when I draw I don't care,
I'll do anything for a dare.

What about the imagery of pornography?
Am I amoral and maybe just giving
the people what they want,
or is it just for the money?
(wouldn't that be funny!)

Art means
never having to say
you're sorry.

Drawings are only a few lines on paper.
Therefore it's easy to carry around in
plastic bags.

Drawings are cheaper than paintings.
They don't pretend that they'll
last forever.

Drawings are streetwise and still
to be found in toilets, too.

The Blonde, the Brunette and the Black Woman

I don't want to sound like Michael Jackson saying
'It don't matter if you're black or white',
because that is, like the issues concerning male and
female, unfortunately still painfully burning bright!
This is a sensitive area for almost everybody.
Yet it is not political correctness that inspired these
images, but the loss of integrity and shifts of identity
that affects everything and most of us, everywere.

These paintings consciously allude to the politics of color
and the color of paintings.
They are even a bit funny. Nothing wrong with
black humour.

I have never experienced paintings as windows or mirrors.
It is impossible to tell what is up and what is down,
who is above and who below. We just don't know.

Is she humiliating him or is he oppressing her?
Is it a prescriptive or a descriptive position?
The blonde, the brunette and the black woman all share
the same snapshot of myself as source material, although
this does not imply selfportraiture. (When the Barbie doll
went into production they made 3 blondes for every one
brunette). The factual information that this type of paintings
have to offer is almost non-existent.

It has been said that you can't judge a book by its cover
and you can't judge a woman by her lover. Yet it seems,
you have to judge a painting by its cover and especially
by its lovers.

Dead Artists

In Europe I eventually discovered the dead artists. Those who were more alive than most of the living ones, like Goya, Holbein, Manet, Degas, and Courbet. Most important I could see them in the flesh. It became clear that (for example) my dislike for Impressionism was based largely on ignorance and prejudice. What I thought (was told, read) was not what I saw.
I do not have artists or painters as heroes. I like and use bits and pieces of many, many artists and non-artists.
I cannot exist without others. They are my audience, my burden, my inspiration, my subjectmatter and objectmatter.

Painting is not in a crisis

Paintings are slow by nature. Someone has to make a painting. It is what it is, through its process of being made. Artistic thinking became psychopathic when it became obsessed with 'the New'. The artworld became ashamed of painting, in a world where speed is power; paintings may look like an area for weak boys to play hide and seek, but as the photographic is losing its shine and becoming yesterdays (News-)papers, yesterdays paintings are smiling.

Drawing is closer

Drawing is closer to whispering into someone's ear, while painting is more like the ear itself. It contains all that has ever entered there. It listens more than it speaks. It throws speech into the dark. Painting is not speechless.
It overflows. It is a drunken mermaid's song.

Women and Painting

I paint because I am a woman.
(It's a logical necessity).
If painting is female and insanity is a female malady, then all women painters are mad and all male painters are women.

I paint because I am an artificial blonde woman.
(Brunettes have no excuse).
If all good painting is about color then bad painting is about having the wrong color. But bad things can be good excuses. As Sharon Stone said, 'Being blonde is a great excuse. When you're having a bad day you can say, I can't help it, I'm just feeling very blonde today.'

I paint because I am a country girl.
(Clever, talented big-city girls don't paint).
I grew up on a wine farm in Southern Africa. When I was a child I drew bikini girls for male guests on the back of their cigarette packs. Now I am a mother and I live in another place that reminds me a lot of a farm – Amsterdam. (It's a good place for painters.) Come to think about it, I'm still busy with those types of images and imagination.

I paint because I am a religious woman.
(I believe in eternity). Painting doesn't freeze time.
It circulates and recycles time like a wheel that turns.
Those who were first might well be last. Painting is a very slow art. It doesn't travel with the speed of light. That's why dead painters shine so bright.
It's okay to be the second sex.
It's okay to be second best.
Painting is not a progressive activity.

I paint because I am an old-fashioned woman.
(I believe in witchcraft).
I don't have Freudian hang-ups. A brush does not remind me of a phallic symbol. If anything, the domestic aspect of a painter's studio (being 'locked up' in a room) reminds me a bit of the housewife with her broom. If you're a witch you will still know how to use it. Otherwise it is obvious that you'll prefer the vacuum cleaner.

I paint because I am a dirty woman.
(Painting is a messy business).
It cannot ever be a pure conceptual medium. The more 'conceptual' or cleaner the art, the more the head can be separated from the body, and the more the labour can be done by others. Painting is the only manual labour I do.

I paint because I like to be bought and sold.
Painting is about the trace of the human touch. It is about the skin of a surface. A painting is not a postcard. The content of a painting cannot be separated from the feel of its surface. Therefore, in spite of everything, Cézanne is more than vegetation and Picasso is more than an anus and Matisse is not a pimp.

It's as easy as 1, 2, 3

One is alone
Two is a couple
Three is politics

How blue can a white Man get?

What's a privileged girl have to be sad about?
What's painters got to be mad about?
Ask me no questions and I'll tell you no lies.
Your expectations are my inspiration.
Your guilt is a big sensation.
Art is a low risk, high-reward crime.

The Muse is exhausted

The muse is exhausted
because she smiles too much.

The muse is exhausted
because she works overtime.
There's too many men and women
that feed from her breasts.

The muse is exhausted
because she has to pour the water
of inspiration, as well as make art
herself and bear children.

The muse is exhausted
because linear time has been
abolished. Everything is here and
now and present tense.

The muse is exhausted
because the nights are never dark
anymore. All that neon confuses the
Night Creatures.They say that owls
and other such animals find it difficult
to sleep because our lights are
everywhere.

The muse is overexposed.
Too much light.

The muse is overloaded.
She is too busy to be reflective.

The muse is overprotected.
Not to be confused with respected.

The muse is pale and melancholic.
An European with a colonial past
and an authoritarian father.

The muse has lost her integrity.
Her tricks have become common
knowledge.

The muse is anachronic.
(Error in computing of time.)

The muse is psychopathic.
She takes too much and
reveals too little.

The muse is famous
too many face lifts, pep pills
and talk shows.

The muse is exhausted
too many bodies and not enough
soul. She's got the porno blues.

Blind Dates and drawn Curtains

<u>What's love got to do with it? What's love but a secondhand emotion?</u>
Tina Turner

I am an artist who uses
secondhand images
and firsthand experiences

If you'll be my blind date
I will be yours

And if we still like one
another in ten years time,
we can call it
love at first sight

The more I paint and draw, or rather, the more exhibitions I have, the less I feel like talking about them beforehand or explaining them afterward. The less I feel like burdening my audiences with food for thought or providing unnecessary (arrogant) crutches to lean on. As if I, by definition, see better than they what I have done. They will not interrogate me and I will not lift up my skirt for inspection, or let the veils fall. Art will not be my slave-market. I will not open my mouth to allow my teeth to be counted by those who count. Art, unlike other love portions, does not induce action. It does not leave torn curtains or bruised lips. Instead of being noisy, it makes you hold your tongue. Instead of making you cry, it freezes your tears. Instead of making you jump up and down, it stops your motion.

It might be exorcism, but it's not revenge. It might be not enough, but it's very close. It might not expose anything, but it draws beautiful curtains.

Art is in love with time. It needs time, it takes time, and it steals time in order to survive in time and be quiet enough to display the silence that betrays everybody and everything.

To Life

The other day,
I read a story about a dwarf
who said that the opposite of
beautiful was not ugly, but death.

Thirteen years ago, I made a work
titled *Love versus Death* and someone
said to me that it was strange that
I did not name life as the opposite
of death, but love.

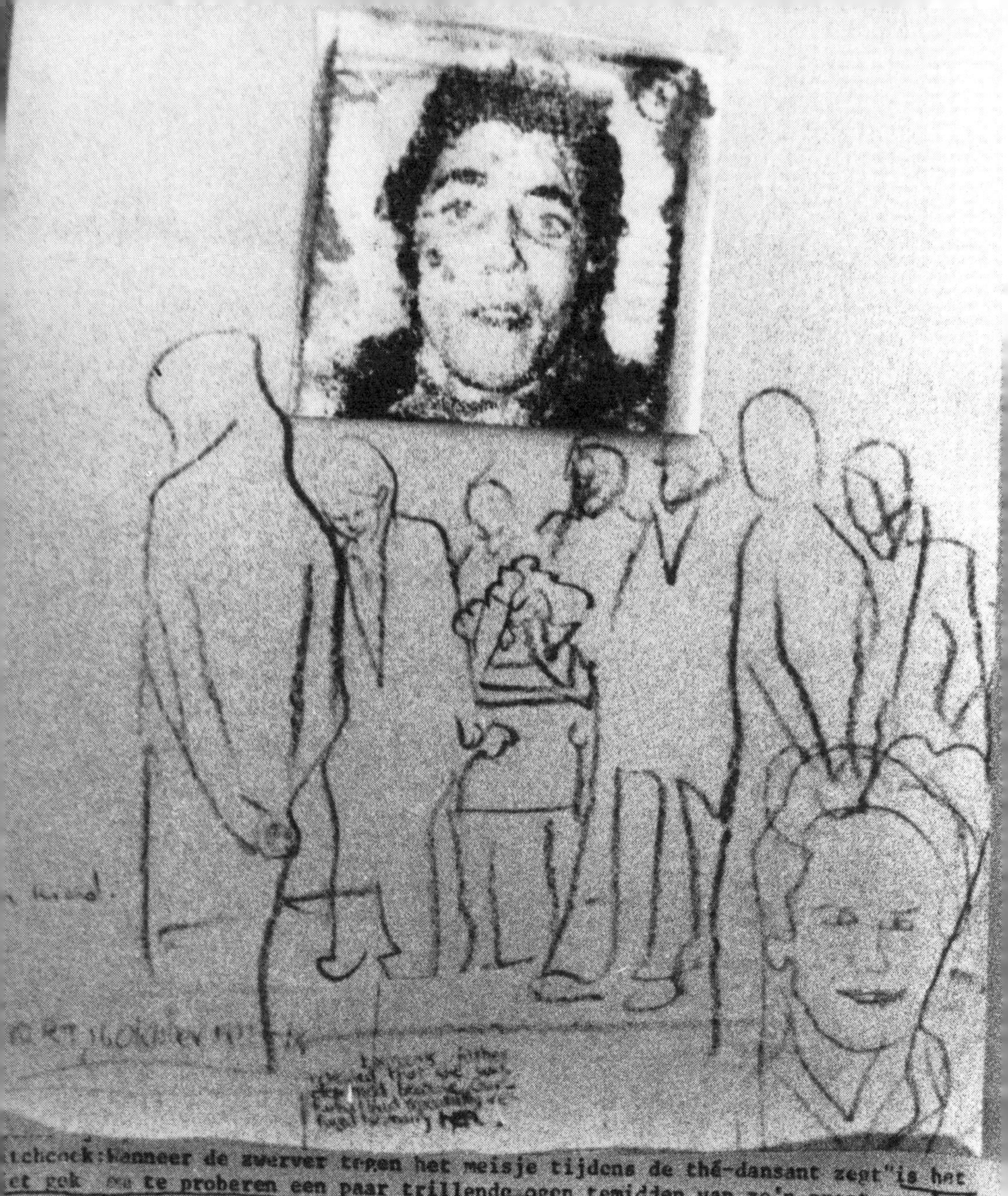

itchcock: Wanneer de zwerver tegen het meisje tijdens de thé-dansant zegt "is het
et gek om te proberen een paar trillende ogen temidden van zo'n groot gezelschap
ontdekken" dan plaats ik op datzelfde moment de kamera in zijn hoogste positie,
de hotel lounge aan het plafond en dan laten we de kamera zakken, door de
bby, de grote balzaal in, langs de dansende mensen, de orkestvloer, de musici
tdat we een close-up hebben van de drummer. De gezichten van de musici zijn
artgeverfd. We blijven bij het gezicht van de drummer totdat zijn ogen het doek
vullen. Dan trillen zijn ogen. Deze hele scène is in één keer opgenomen.

t "Hitchcock by François Truffaut" Panther Books 1967.

Home is where the Heart is

My fatherland is South Africa
my mothertongue is Afrikaans
my surname is French.
I don't speak French.
My mother always wanted me to go to Paris
she thought Art was French,
because of Picasso.
I thought Art was American,
because of Artforum.
I thought Mondriaan was American too,
and that Belgium was a part of Holland.
I live in Amsterdam
and have a Dutch passport.
Sometimes I think I'm not a real artist,
because I'm too half-hearted;
and I never quite know where I am.

Dutch Art?

For me the questions are:

Why be placed, and why allow myself to be placed in an exhibition of Dutch Art in Paris, when I do not see myself as a Dutch Artist? Why do I live in Holland (for almost 18 years now) since 5 years with a Dutch passport, and not see myself as Dutch? And why participate in groupshows, if one does not form a group. Because I am scared, I'm a coward, I'm an opportunist and I'm lonely.

Thinking about myself in a Dutch context cannot be done without thinking about South Africa. Now, that is enough to make one sick, which is just what I am at the moment! I am grateful that the Dutch took me in. It gave me a place to rest, like a psychiatric couch on which to lay comfortable, while one's nightmares are exposed. It's socio-political system has been good to me as an artist, and as a woman. South Africa though remains my cruel muse and judge, which like the christian God cannot be appeased. While the Dutch take my hand and tell me I'm ok. Holland allowed me to paint, because they believe in painting.

I could say – South Africa is my content and Holland is my form, but then, the images I deal with are familiar to almost everyone, everywhere. I deal with second-hand images and first-hand experiences. (My 'models' have all already modelled for someone else. There aint no virgins here.) And my medium is ancient too. Through art nothing gets solved, so everything remains relevant. 'Contemporary' issues are older than time – the body, the other, trans-cultural objects, placelessness, flatness, the sexual organs of the snail, everything is related.

I don't know much about geography but I know that for me French art is still BB. Brigitte Bardot, Buren, Boltansky and Bustamante.

Not from Here (I)

The young child, the painter,
the foreigner are 'not from here',
they are often not part of the ruling
discourse, the preconceptions that
are common or fashionable at a
certain stage.

I am NOT a New Yorker
I am NOT Dutch
I am NO longer living in South Africa.

I am always 'not from here',
even though I try to know
or understand 'what's going on' and
what the rules are and how they
keep on changing and what that means.
When looking at images I'm not lost,
but I'm uneasy.

Not from Here (II)

In a time when we are so aware (or seem to be) of what happens in the world through TV, newspapers and other photobased mediums, painting that refers in one way or another to these issues steps into a whole arena of misunderstanding, especially when the painter uses recognizable images of the human figure. It is however a very exciting place to be in. Because painted human figures remain always imagined beings, that have their own peculiar features and psychology. They are closer to the world of ghosts and angels, daydreams and nightmares than to real people in the streets. In a sense they are always 'not from here', which does not mean that they don't play with our sexual fantasies and fears, and our political preconceptions. They are fully aware of them. They exploit them and smile at our discomfort and quest for straightforward meanings.

They know how often evil travels in straight lines. Paintings are silent things. They don't tell us what to do. They do not force themselves upon you as the more theatrical mediums do. That is why painting is often seen as dead, compared to the more noisy art forms. Paintings are like frogs, if you don't kiss them, there can be no love story. And even then you can never know beforehand, beyond doubt, what type of frog you're dealing with. (ugh.) Paintings don't die. They only go to sleep when no one looks at them.

Blackbirds and young boys

In my exhibition *Not from Here*[1] there's black and white as races. And there's black and white as colors. There's pink bodies and darkblue faces. There's black people who are yellow and white people who are dark and skins peeling off and eyes left out. And sometimes it's also a little bit funny.

1 Jack Tilton Gallery, New York, 11.5 – 18.6.1994

The secret

The painting is the secret.
The painting is not a
pervert with a rain coat.
It turns its back on you,
and minds it's own business.

Night time

Night time is the right
time (as the song goes).
In the dark all people
look the same. Yet the
darkness is not always
the same. The night has
many colours.

My first exhibition of only (portrait)
paintings, in Holland, was called
The Eyes of the Night Creatures.

Betrayal

or the art of reading faces.
There is no way to spot
the odd one out. The rotten spot,
the bad woman, because we are all
under suspicion: as Jean Genet said:
'because life contains these erotic
conditions I was bent on evil.'
(We try to read our tea cups and
hands to know what will happen, but
we cannot fortell our own fate.)
I won't point my finger to you,
'cause I don't know who's to blame.

Cupid

'Don't you mess with
cupid, 'cause Cupid ain't
stupid'. The young child is so sensual
and gentle at times that it scares me.
My daughter (5 years now)
shows me her body without
posing to please.
She shows me the cruelty
and magic of innocence.
Not every image I paint
was inspired by her though.

Reinhardts Daughter

You change the colour
of something and
everything changes
(especially if you're a painter).

The Hatred of Others

Art may lie
love may die
but hatred remains
a lasting sentiment.
Forgiveness ain't easy,
even God, admits that.
He first had to kill his own son
to see the light.

I used to have a quote by
Jean Paul Sartre in my sketchbook in
artschool in the 70's that read:
'The Hatred of others reveals to me,
my own objectivity.'

If you really want
to talk to others,
get a good translator

Jesus

The perfect lover
what more is there to say.

St. Mark, chapter 14:
'And the second time the cock crew
and Peter called to mind the words
that Jesus said unto him,
"Before the cock crows twice,
thou shalt deny me twice".
And when he thought there-on, he wept'.

If loving you is wrong, I don't want to be right
Luther Ingram

Lovesick

Green, ghosts, good, God, gone, glow.

I used to think that there was something unusual about my work. I always tried to show that there was something wrong, where others thought everything was allright.

Now, while I sometimes feel that things ain't that bad all the time, everyone else says that it's much worse. It seems nobody really feels that life is allright. Everyone is looking for abuse and new laws on pornography, especially since 'the artworld' dicovered 'the body' (whatever that means). Ask Courbet, since he is credited, or blamed, for discovering the source.

I used to prefer: hard to soft, black to white, the Rolling Stones to the Beatles, Elvis to Cliff, the moon to the sun... (I still do actually.)

I haven't outgrown my tendencies towards uneasiness, anger, aggression, deep and cheap horror, falling in and out of love...

But there has to be a way to make an art about being in love. An art that is erotic, sexy, tender and filled with a darkness that is awesome, but not sick.

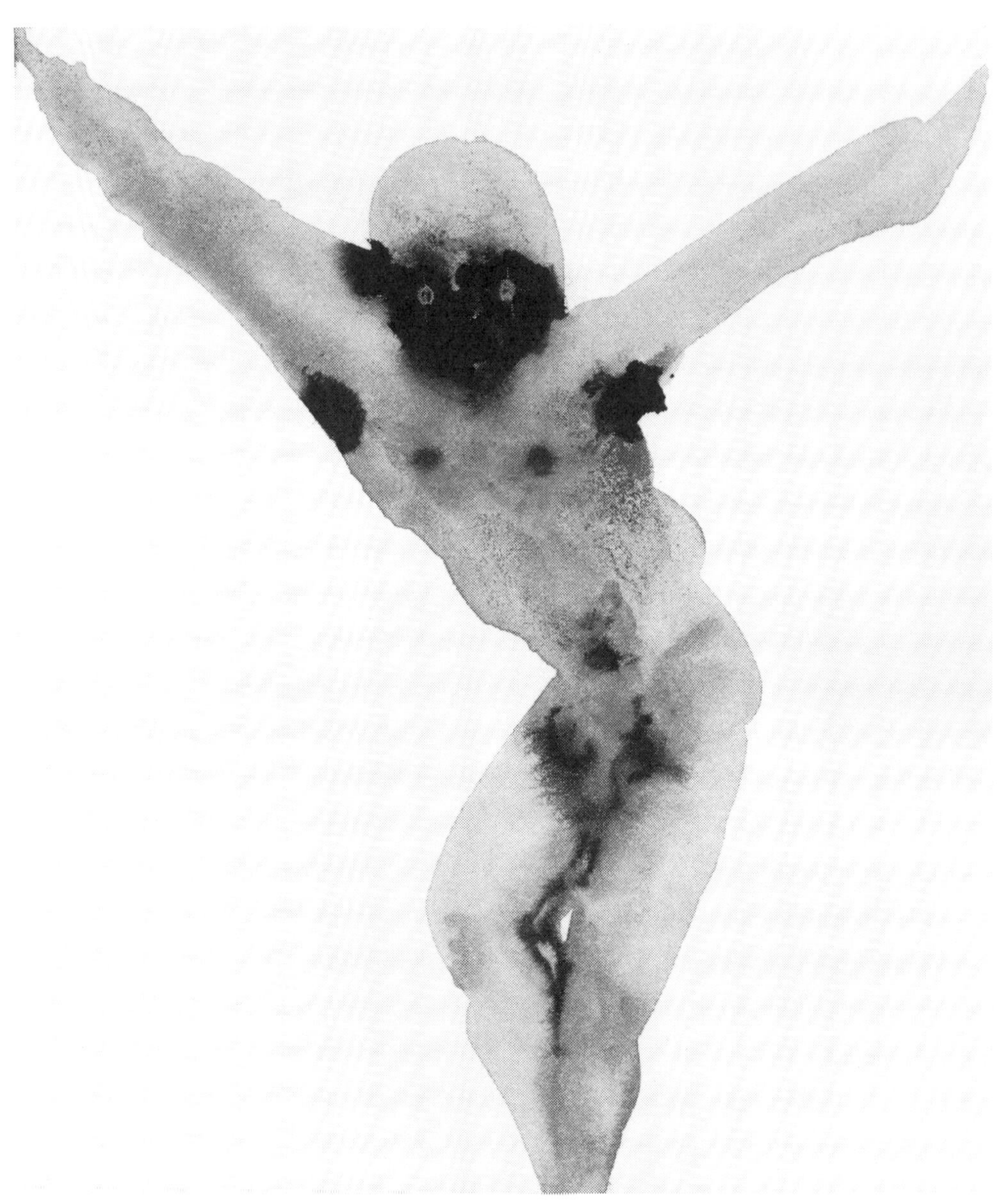

Jesus (sketch for the perfect Lover) 1994

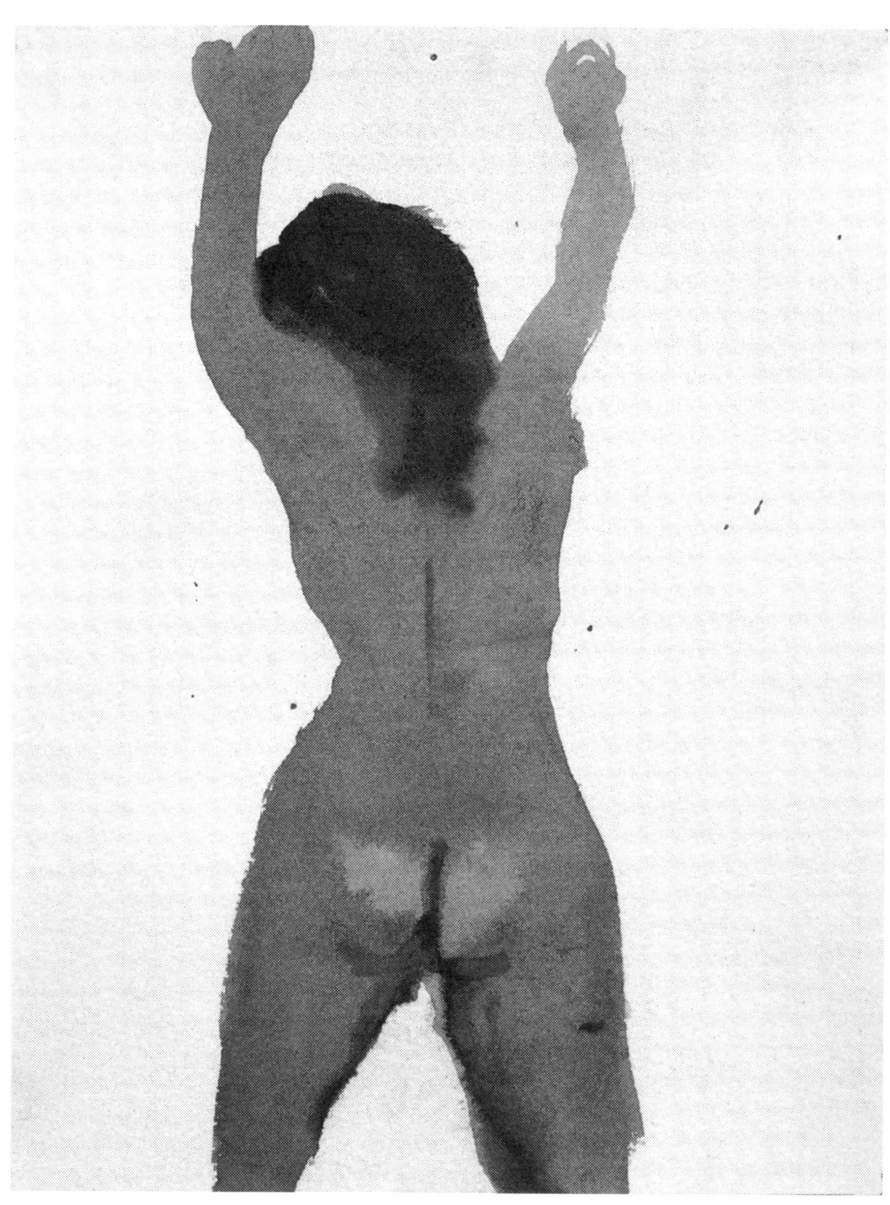

Chlorosis (Lovesick) 1994

The beginning of Love Stories and the End of cultural Privacy

Identity

Don't use the word identity in my presence. For years a political system (in South Africa) insisted that what they've done, they've had to do to protect my identity.

Others

Yes, I am fascinated by the exotic, and the erotic and the barbaric and the heroic.
Yes. I am scared of Black people.
Yes I am scared of white people and dead people and sick people and especially those who say they like my work.

Raw and cooked

A Fisherman caught a mermaid, took her home to his family and called the TV people to come and record this catch. But when they all rushed in to view this sensation, the grandmother had put her in a pot and cooked her for dinner.

Transcultural

I've always loved sad men, images of naked women, mermaids, God, tombstones and the smell of gasoline...

The next Generation

When Black and White are colours
and not races, people will still fall in
love and discriminate between
partners and feel sad and bad
and need art that breaks your heart
and takes you to those places
where pain becomes beauty.

Beyond the Protection of the Law

Art doesn't want to sleep with you
Art ain't that good
and
Art ain't that nice
Art makes you feel cold
and
Art declares you a fugitive

Three Maria's are better than One

The Model, the Muse, the Slave and the Patron Saint of Hairdressers

When once asked to comment on the matter,
I said that the Muse was tired.
And – yes, indeed –
everybody needs a break now and then.
But 'tired' does not mean 'exhausted',
and it definitely doesn't mean 'dead'.

She's well paid and satisfied.
She knows she's got what you ain't got.
She knows how to keep secrets
and how to show that she's got some.

She's got the power to withhold information,
to refrain from confession,
to abstain from need.
And if you tell her she's got a beautiful body,
she would not hold it against you.

Apparitions and Illusions or 'kill the Moonlight'

I have once written:
between the motif
and the traces of the hand
falls the shadow.

Now I'd like to add:
between the model and the source,
between the source and the act,
between the act and the consequences,
iconography becomes self-deception.

Models

Magdalena
or the Megamodel meets the holy Whore

It's not the fallen woman
nor the temptress I'm after.
It's not the babydolls I want
nor the Amazons. It's everything
mixed together to form
a true bastard race.

Painting is my oldest subject
Fashion is my newest
and Beauty is my youngest.

On Beauty

(They say) Art no longer produces Beauty,
She produces meaning, but

(I say) One cannot paint a picture,
or make an image of a woman
and not deal with the concept of beauty.

A Queen of Spades[1]

Where does the Black Model
come from?
Some dark
blue place
where the sun always shines?
From an old African
postcard and Naomi Campbell's
legs in Vogue.
From the city
from her liking
crowds
and hating
solitude.
From Giacometti,
from the brothel
in Avignon,
from Mary
of Egypt,
from everywhere
these days.

1 That's what Courbet called Manet's *Olympia*

A fair(ly) synthesized Maid

Where does the White Model
come from?
From a cool, transparent place
called Western Art?
From the club of broken hearts.
From a city where it rains
all the time.
She is a North European
Magdalena called Heidi.
She is my attempt
to equal Barnett Newman's zip.
Not so much his straight-edge zip,
but his frayed-edge zip.
She is not 'ravaged by space'.[1]
She is just spaced-out
most of the time.

1 'The flatness of flat is something we've solved', Barnett Newman

Supernatural

What happened to
our animal nature?
It ended up on the
catwalk.

I wanted to LOOK like
Twiggy and the Shrimp.
Later I tried to THINK
like Simone de Beauvoir
and BE like the boys.

Out of Eggs, out of Business[1]

I'm now getting
into the Middles Ages.
I'd like to dry up gracefully
like the saints.

Beuys demanded that one shows one's wounds
and Degas demanded that a woman had that touch
of ugliness without which there is no salvation.

1 Lauren Hutton in an interview with Dennis Hopper on modelling and aging

A pai
needs
to obj

nting
a wall
ect to

The wrong Questions

If you ask the wrong questions
you can't get the right answers.

I don't have no fin-de-siècle desperation.
I don't like to 'take a stand'.
I'd rather fly and create distance
because that is what the intellect does and should do.

Art doesn't point fingers or serve 'the good'.
Art is and should stay as AMORAL as possible.

Artists should (re)consider their AESTHETIC consciousness;
their ETHICAL consciousness is mostly not that interesting
at all – if not a drawback.

Art partakes in Evil and whatever Beauty sees.

Goya's The Fates

It has always saddened me that the artform that chose me as its mistress did not make people cry. Music does. Books do. And bad movies do it even better. But not paintings.

There are some good explanations for this. Paintings don't move. They don't have the same type of narrative structure or succession of time as the moving pictures. There's no build-up of tensions and release, like in a thriller. You see too much, all at once. Good paintings are made by the grace of their well-measured sense of distance. This distancing of affections makes them tough enough to outlast their time, but also too cool and controlled for the cheaper sensational thrill of moving someone to tears. When I saw the Prado for the first time, I stood in awe in front of Velazquez and I could see why he is considered the greatest European painter.

But I did not cry.

Then I walked into the room with Goya's black paintings, they put their spell on me. I covered my mouth as if to prevent the devil from entering. *The Fates* does away with the abstraction versus figuration discussion. Everything is flat and deep simultaniously. The four sexually ill-defined figures are unsympathetic. They are forces, not human beings. It is as if he painted not the screams of humanity, but rather the silence of God.

I felt so alone and yet so at home. I bathed in this sensuous, ominous brew of ritualism and exorcism. I felt the Gypsies, Islam, Christianity and Africa, all at the same time.

And then I cried.

The perfect Lover, the absent Lover and the Daughter

Complicity

I experience human beings as very untrustworthy creatures, because even if not consciously or deliberately, they do much harm to one another. The psychological harm, more than the physical violence, interests me. The tension between two subjects or the tension between an individual and a group fascinates me. The point where attraction and distrust meet, for example in movies like *The Invasion of the Body Snatchers*. You see how loved ones and friends still look the same, but are actually aliens with bad intentions. The title of my selfportrait *Evil is banal* (1984) relates to these issues too. Everyone is potentially capable of extreme cruelty, if the circumstances feed it enough. The dark-haired stepmother can be a wonderful person, while the soft-spoken blonde mother could be the witch. We don't (can't) know what is going to happen, at the first glance.

But the question is not so much: Is the other person good or bad? (or this or that), but: Who are we? For Oscar Wilde the final mystery is one-self. When I'm attracted to someone and especially when it's an erotic attraction, I'm struck by the complexity of my emotions. It's a mixture of beauty, vulnerability, love, fear and disgust, almost simultaneously.

But how to paint or draw that?

Firstly, I have to be sensually attracted to my subject matter. There is no need for a real person. Naomi Campbell's image fascinates me, especially how she uses those lips! (I don't particulary want to meet her at all.)

Because I use photographs as source material for my compositions, the choice of the right (appropriate) image is very important. The image has to carry the possi-billity of being able to be transformed into my medium (water and ink or oil on canvas). I'm not trying to imitate the photograph. I use the photograph. The photographic illusionism that the drawings or paintings display makes strong references to the real world outside of the artwork.

At the same time, the medium (the colors, textures and the brush strokes and gestures) has to have a lot of freedom too, so it can run into its own paths of chance and suprise. I take pure joy in the making and the material qualities of the work. Even if the work uses 'sad' images (the 'what' may be painful, but the 'how' is always joyful). The work is not manic, nor depressive. The 'how' smiles at the 'what'. There is nothing as funny as unhappiness says Samuel Beckett. This is my sense of humor.

The balance between control and letting go is very important. Deliberation meets arbitrariness. There is not a set message to decipher, there is ambiguousness to come to terms with, an existential awareness that the interpretation of my work operates like a movie with an open ending. We do not know if Scarlett got Rett Butler back in *Gone with the Wind*. There is no way of knowing this. We have to live in a state of tension. And with single images (even if the drawings have more parts) we have even less information to help us form our opinions about what it could mean. Or worse – 'should' mean.

Audience

The audience is part of the meaning-making process. It's prejudices are part of it's enjoying or rejecting of the images. Therefore the audience is an accomplice in completing 'the story'. The audience can't get away by saying 'I don't know anything about art, but I know what I like'. It might be true, but it's not an excuse, because the work is also about the interaction of art (rules of a specialized game) and that what one really likes or believes in regardless. The images confront the viewer mostly by looking at them, thus showing an awareness of being looked at. In a way 'asking' for a reaction. One can only look one person in the eyes at a particular moment. Therefore this feeling of intimacy. This is between the two of you. You can do with each other what you like, and yet the image also has a judging ability. A distance; like something to protect you from the evil eye, but that could also deliver you to the wrong party, if you make the wrong move. I put myself on equal footing with the subjects. You (the viewer) or I do not have to feel sorry for my subjects, as if you are 'better off' than they are. The relationship is between equals.

No neutrality

I use all the cheap tricks of attracting attention: eyes looking at you, sexual parts exposed or deliberately covered. The primitive pull of recognition. The image as prostitute. You are forced to say yes or no.

Roots

My works mostly reveal their roots in their titles, which give an idea where these people are coming from. But in the groups of portrait heads I do treat the faces with a certain equality. The sane look a bit crazy, and the crazy look sane, and everybody is trying to seduce you in some way or another. And everyone has got a bit of high and low in them, and don't really care too much about pleasing you.

Black women

Most of the famous paintings we know are done by white males and made 'of' white female models. When one acknowledges the beauty of black women (and men) it becomes unnatural to exclude them. The fact that it gets extra attention just shows one how white the art world still is around here.

Background

My South African background will always remain present. But the word-image relation in my work not only has to do with that and is not only from there. The whole artworld relies on words to defend, explain or authorize artworks. Look at the many catalogues, art magazines and artbooks making works 'accessible' or giving them a context for being important. I never believed that an artwork could only be 'optical'. One 'learns' to see as you learn to read. I don't however, mean that it's the same activity or that artworks have only literal meanings. What you read makes you 'see' differently and vice versa. Cinema uses text and images together, or disturbes them like Godard, as part of its natural history. Why shouldn't painting?

Portrait heads

The groups of portrait heads are very addictive. One can't stop once started. It's as if one wants everyone you have ever met or seen, to be touched by your hand. The dead and the living. Sometimes I get scared that it can become too obsessive and that one can't get out of this trance. Everyone is different and yet quite similar. All discrimination becomes senseless and useless. The notion of good and bad drawings also disappears.

Chlorosis

Chlorosis (1994) has been described as portraits of only women. That is not true. A picture of Johnny Rotten (Sex Pistols) has been used as a model; and some other male artists too. I made this group after my group *Jesus Serene* (1994), in which I deliberately tried not to use strong black and white contrasts. I wanted to see if I could still make compelling images without using the dramatic effects of dark and light juxtapositions. Also the expressions of Jesus had to be very absent, as if he looked through you. A don't-touch-me feeling, because 'I am not from here anymore and I am not interested in physical sensuality, only in spiritual sensuality'. Yet one still had to feel attracted to this 'man', even though he did not want you as 'a woman' or as a material presence. I used very light or pale colours of pink, yellow, blue, green etc. At times I thought it was just too soft and kitsch, to be still called a 'strong' work.

Chlorosis then continued with this paleness. Now, mostly greenisch, longing, without the extreme extacy of St.Theresa, but with a fever inside. I wanted it to vibrate like a sad love song. Singing like a type of Ophelia slowly losing her mind from sadness. It was so close and yet in a way the opposite of the Jesus drawings. They longed for him, the perfect lover. Because of his absence, perfection was not betrayed. Yet neither was satisfaction obtained.

Mary Magdalena

From *Chlorosis* to *Mary Magdalena* (1996) was easy, even logical. I called them only Magdalena, to make it less historically religious. I also liked the fact that this woman wants the man and he says 'no'. My men are often supposedly feminine, while my women are more masculine (if you still want to use this distinction). I believe in love-stories. The gender of the lovers does not matter in the end. The religous connotations are like my use of fairy tale figures: to give the public an easy startingpoint. A popular reference that relates to all times and that's familiar to most people. For non-christian people it's easy to look at too, because they are looking at a strong, yet vulnerable female image (she's naked), that looks back at them, even if they don't know her name. The Magdalena's were constructed by using parts of supermodels' bodies and parts (and poses) of old paintings of women. It's like Madonna chosing this name for her singing career. She's not trying to be the real Madonna from the bible, but it helps.

Underground

Helena decorated, improved and worked on my black and white drawings with colour when she was six years old.[1] She found them a bit too boring. I was her underground. Unlike Arnulf Rainer working on photographs, she worked 'against' me rather. I allowed her to play with my drawings so I could do other work. This wasn't set up as an art project in the first place. She 'recasted' my models into her own stories. One was kidnapped, she said, and walked into a horse.

Helena said: 'It's easier to draw sick people.
You give them a wound,
you make them cry,
and then you give them a band-aid'.

1 *Underground* 1994–95, Marlene Dumas and Helena

Pin-Up

Can pin-ups still survive in a pornographic age?
Somehow just like marriage and prisons they still do.

Origin

The pin-up is of American/English origin. As is the word 'sexy'. It dates from somewhere around the beginning of the century. In Europe there were more pornographic pictures. These didn't exist in America. As a very young girl I drew those cheerful cliches, copied from comic strips and cartoons. I often drew them on the backs of cigarette packets of friends who came to visit my parents. I made these sketches very quickly and they turned out differently every time, yet somehow the same. And so everyone was very impressed and assured me that I was destined for the arts.

A classic pin-up is primarily fantasy and never actually intended to be touched or possessed.

I always wanted a sailor.
So I could long for him
while he's gone.
And be happy when he comes.

Softcore yet tough.
Pink puff
hot stuff
she's had enough.

With regret for the fact
that 'sexy' also implies something stupid
and the fine arts avoid that
in favour of the 'erotic'.
I've always felt related to those places
where the pin-up feels at home.
And I thank all those nameless artists
who've given us the real pin-ups.

Youth and other Demons

When I think of youth,
I think of
the New People of Japan,
the film Death in Venice,
the paintings of Saint Sebastian,
the woodblock prints of blue-ish spirits,
my own youth – becoming a ghost.

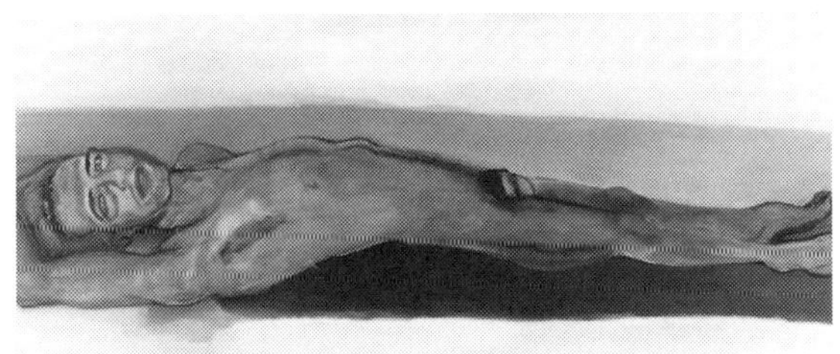

Particularity of Nakedness 1987 140 x 300 cm

Masterpieces and Miss World

The fairest in the land
is not the fairest on the wall

When I was young all the Miss Worlds looked alike. No Chinese or black Ghanese or Japanese ever won. It was always a white American type that was found the fairest, although the other countries were allowed to participate, which gave the event a more international feel. In relation to artworks everyone thinks and accepts that many different points of view can and even should justifiably exist next to each other.

And yet we still end up asking the question who is the best or the most beautiful; or what painting of the future will look like. No-one wants to believe that in principle nothing 'has to' but everything 'could'.

We want beauty to be imitable. And seeing that judgements are made by people, there's something to be said for that. Between 'Only the marvellous is beautiful' of André Breton and 'All is pretty' of Andy Warhol, I stand.

What do I want?

I want a bit of everything. Sometimes I want more of this and less of that and sometimes an overload of the other is also wonderful. I don't become a better person, through this, only fuller and more needy.

First Flights Overseas

I came to Holland
at the age of 23
to see American art.
I missed South-Africa
and often felt very lonely.
Here are some of the lines written then.

Holland 1977

I'm as cold inside myself today
as some Hitler's mistress somewhere.
Apart from that
it's 'quite a nice day'.

Doomed to room

We are doomed doomed to rooms
where we watch motionless
the motionless done works of others
behind glass and/or other
transparent materials.

Rejects and Reasons

In South-Africa you have Reject Stores. They sell clothes that have flaws or some imperfections. It makes them cheaper.

Every group discriminates. They kick out those they feel don't fit in; or leave out others because of a limited amount of space (or other reasons).

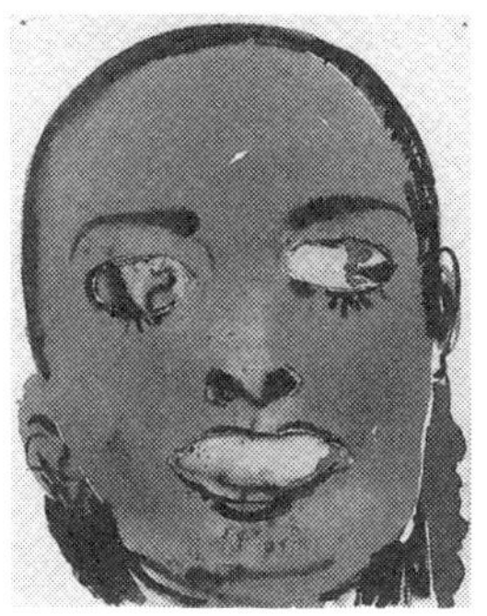

Rejects (detail) 1994 60 x 50 cm

I'd rather be abused than rejected

Andries Botha

Art and Prostitution

If – a prostitute is a person
who makes it a profession
to gratify the lust of various persons
for economical reasons or gain,
where emotional involvement may
or may not be present;

Then – it seems not so far removed
from my definition of an artist.
Artists usually love to pretend.
Artists usually pretend to love
much more than they can handle.
They want everyone to want them
while they don't want anybody.

I'm not really bad – I'm just drawn that way
Jessica Rabbit

What's a nice Girl like you doing in a Place like this

I'm not looking for trouble
I don't go and mess about
with ethno-things and images
or identity-politics and multi- and poly-issues;
I'll take nothing less than a
supermodel.
So there can be no blame, concerning
the misuse of innocent victims,
she's so much more beautiful
so much richer, and so much
more powerful than me,
so much for equality.

The Drive-Inn

It was film
that taught me the rules of the imagination
not reality
nor painting.

Women

I have painted more women
than men
I paint women for men
I paint women for women
I paint the women of my men.

As the World turns

Vollard said, 'Of course ordinarily a portrait of a woman is always more expensive than a portrait of a man, but,' said he, looking at the picture very carefully, 'I suppose with Cezanne it doesn't make any difference'.

Valentines Day

Why do I so often write in the style of love about art? Because the talk of forbidden lovers and the language of art have a lot in common.

Love is the most wonderful when it has to live in secret, when it isn't really allowed; when it is sanctioned by everyone, and the lovers now officially belong together, it's nature changes.

Secret love knows that it is almost always time to go. Other loves have their fears too, but then they believe they have the right to be jealous. But if you're 'wrong' to start off with, you can't speak of having 'rights'. You understand that if the beloved leaves, it's because that is how it 'should' be.

With art the best part is when you make something that seems to be against what you thought you believed in. And yet, you know that that's what you want.

René Magritte on love: 'A man is privileged when his passions oblige him to betray his convictions to please the woman he loves.'

Always true

Why do I want my texts to be read?
Why do I keep on coming back on what I've said?
Why all the fuss and I'm not even dead?

Because people keep on asking me
the same old things, and I can't remember
what I've said, if I don't see it as words to be read.

Never mind if it is art, or smart,
but it is true?
True to what?
True to you, of course.

'My baby whispers in my ear
mmmmm... Sweet Nothings...
He knows the things I like to hear...'

Accepting Painting for what it is

When I was at art school I wanted painting to have a stronger connection to reality, to be more like 'real life'. I wanted to be a photographer because I thought it was closer to real life. People who made paintings or fantasy images where figures floated in the air were removed from reality, I thought. Perfomance artists seemed closer to the real thing. Why make an enormous painting in order to tell you that I love you when I can simply write you a letter? But I really love to make images with my hands, so to resolve this contradiction, I started to make use of all the things that bothered me about painting. I realised that I don't want to make a human being. I'm not God. I'm making something else. When I started to embrace the ambiguity of the image, and accepted the realisation that the image can only come to life through the viewer looking at it, and that it takes on meaning through the process of looking, I began to accept painting for what it was.

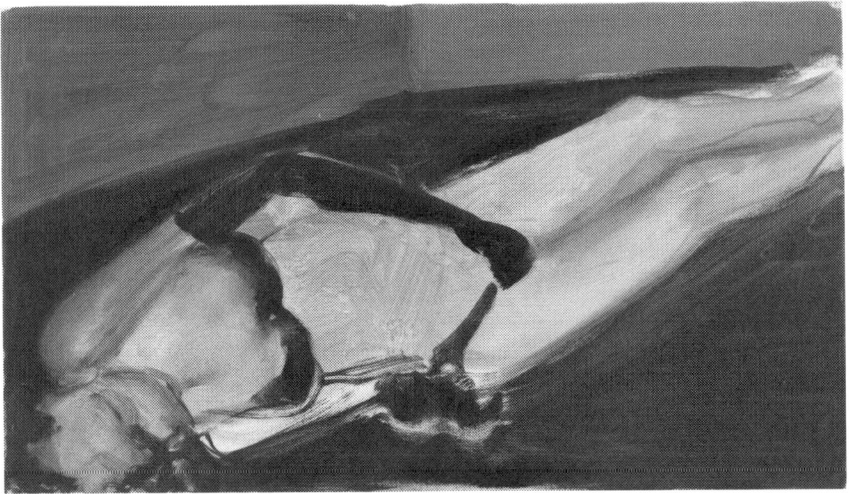

Suspect 1999 56 x 100 cm

Improper Relationships

If you can identify with 'the pictures' generation
and with those who've seen more reel love than real love
and if you can appreciate *Stage*[1],
where the two shall never meet,
because they were in different scenes and on separate screens all along;
you realize that in the beginning was not the word, nor the flesh
but the Editor, who cut the frames, who gave the names and said,
'Not tonight, Josephine.'

1 *Stage*, 1996, a short film by Steve McQueen (black-and-white film, transferred to video, no sound, 6 min., loop).

A true Hedonist is hard to find

Or, what Dolly Parton replied when asked,
'Do you think you'll get out of showbusiness and just do God's work?'
'Well, God and I have a great relationship, we both see other people.'

I was always concerned about what God would want me to do.
I always wondered if art was good enough for God and if so,
what subject matter would be worth pursuing. I knew sexy was low,
erotic a bit higher and sorrow the noblest.

I was told that I belonged to the Western, European tradition, a tradition imbued with the Christian notion that human life is a fall from grace.

I was told that Oriental and African erotica sprang from a source so different and alien that I would not understand it.

But why on earth should I instinctively prefer the Greeks to the Columbians? Why should I prefer the Great American Nude to the early Taoist love manuals and why am I supposed to feel closer to Leda and the Swan than to the Japanese shunga?

I now believe that if I could combine the hedonism of Matisse with the eroticism of Picasso I'd be a happy woman. However, if I could add the divine sensuality of the Hindu temple goddesses of India, I'd be in heaven.

MD-light

It's the pleasures of painting
the poses of pleasure
the privilege of being looked at
the ploys of seduction
the light of the night
it's nothing personal
it's plain delight.

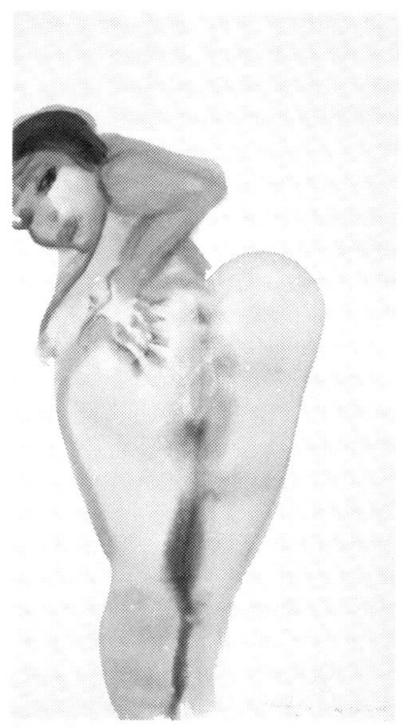

Mandy 1998 125 x 70 cm

Fame and Fortune

You can't get away
from the people you don't like
because they pay for you.

Never say Never, or One Drawing too Many

Serial Killers

I am never going to make a series of heads again, or for that matter a group of similar yet different things placed next to or (too) close to one another. It is effective – it's not just drawing, it's an installation. You are not just facing one image in front of you, you are surrounded. You stand among them. But while it is effective, it is irritating at the same time. You cannot look at just one, without the others bothering you with their indifferences. As in a neurotic (not erotic) movie, the ex-husband always turns up to remind you that he's just as good as (or in American films – always better than) the love of the moment. So whoever she chooses – it leaves a sense of incompleteness, always the awareness that there is more than one. It's not that less is a bore, but more is not enough.

Miss Europe goes to America

This is the first time my Models are to be shown in America. Among other things, they speak about how to make a beautiful drawing of beautiful subject matter. As drawings they are refined, delicate, direct and immediate. As subjects my source material has crossed many centuries. I like to travel in time, to tear out pictures and make them mine, to take other people's muses and make them mine. The spirit of their former master and mistress still linger among them, but now these ghosts are mine. They represent a type of European rather than American stream of consciousness. I do Bardot and not Monroe.

One more time

A drawing is much faster than a fashion shoot. You don't need a room full of hairdressers, stylists and make-up artists. You do it all alone. You don't even need the model either. Rejects are not pictures of injured bodies or battered wives, although the rough and careless handling they have suffered gives them an 'abused' touch. They are about my conflicting attitudes towards drawing and I do have a tendency to want to destroy what I've made. To me this comes more naturally than adhering to a consciously controlled system, so in this sense Rejects are easy and Models difficult. (Models are closer to Robert Ryman and Rejects to Arnulf Rainer – if these gentlemen can forgive these skin-deep comparisons). I am forever torn between wanting a clear simple form that aspires to stand up forever and a reasonless disappearance into formlessness. Rejects enjoy the irresponsible freedom of constantly changing one's mind. No Reject becomes a Model, but every Model fears rejection.

Name no Names

Prisoners are told that torture will stop if they talk. But the rule rather than the exception is that after they've talked, they are killed anyway.

Names are a means of distinguishing people, you from others, serving different purposes in different fields. A name is an identifying device. You can't get the papers you might need if you don't have a passport and you can't get a passport if you don't have a name (but you don't want your name if your name ain't no good).

Relatives Names link you to others with similar names. I thought I was related to Alexandre Dumas with his three musketeers, Camelia and the iron mask . I was wrong. It's unclear if my ancestors who came to the Cape (of Good Hope) somewhere in the 1600's were French Huguenots (religious refugees that is), or just plain criminals.

Naming A child beginning to speak starts by naming things. The God of the Bible makes a big point of naming others but 'He' cannot be named. 'I am' is enough for the Divine. When a person becomes well-known the status of their name changes and people ask if they can 'use your name'. But you can't give it to everyone, otherwise the magic wears off.

Renaming One of the first acts of conquerors is to rename. When people are sold as slaves, they are given new names by their owners and during the Vietnam War (to name just one) names of places were changed and numbered. The instances in history where names turned into numbers are too numerous to recount. I seldom throw drawings away. They may wait for years to be reworked, integrated into other works, or just to be re-named.

Last Names Cassius Clay became Muhammad Ali. It was a positive act, religious and political. When married, most women take their husband's surname to emphasise the fact that she is now supposed to be one with him. Many entertainers and criminals have double names, reflecting their double lives. Lovers have nicknames for each other. Untitled artworks end up having nicknames too.

Strangers have to introduce themselves. Animals start sniffing at one another; people ask for credentials. I once saw a movie about Samson and Delilah. As she stepped out of the water, he asked, 'Who are you?' She replied, 'Who do you want me to be?' They both made a mistake.

Forget Love and art used to be the places where all of this could be forgotten, disappear, break down. As Paul Valéry said, 'seeing is when you forget the name of the thing at which you are looking'. That can be a frightening and alienating experience if you're an anxious existentialist. But it could it also be a wonderful ego-vanishing sensation – a liberation from prejudice and retrospection.
Why do I draw? Is it to remember or to forget?

First Names A child can draw before he can write. The child's doubt about what it is he's doing is not there from the start, the critical moment for the child and his drawing arises, when he writes his name for the first time and the letters still struggle to represent themselves as autonomous shapes, instead of referring to something else. After that moment, drawing and writing each go their own way. I don't long for childhood or innocence lost, even though some of the most touching drawings have been made by children, mental patients and prisoners.

Ashes to Ashes The first time I was invited to send drawings to an international drawing exhibition was in 1981. Almost all the drawings and the whole Galeria Nacional de Arte Moderna in Lisbon were completely destroyed by fire, after which the catalogue listed works that didn't exist anymore. In his essay Donald Kuspit wrote about the return of the child's drawing and more importantly, he described how most of the works had a "double dealing" look about them. For whatever it's worth, one of my drawings was called, It's not My Fault.

Like a Chinese Whatever else my drawings speak of, they are about the vitality of gesture, speed and action. I would like to make the one-stroke, ink brush paintings to which the ancient Chinese aspired. They called it painting and we call it drawing.

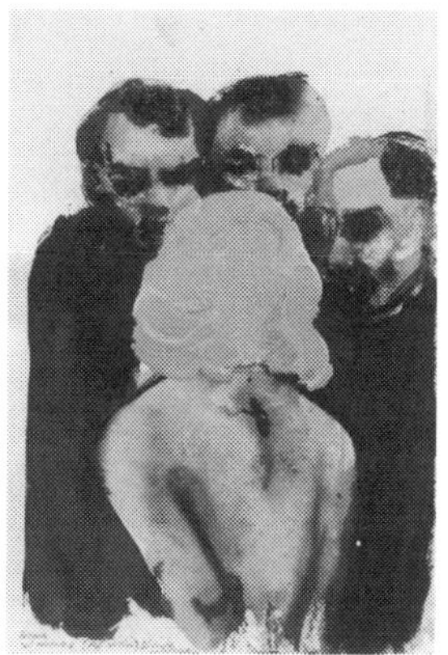

Name no Names 2005 31 x 21,5 cm

Topless Bars and Structural Skeletons
(it's not a Grid, it's an Irritation)

I don't do straight lines. But I've come to realize that sporadically, over the years, bar-like structures emerge every time I try to express intense feelings of frustration regarding the limitations of art and life.

See what happens in All is Fair in Love and War[1]. Twenty years later and here we go again: the politics of geometry versus the geography of politics – figures caught in jail-like trappings.

1 Dumas refers to the exhibition *All is Fair in Love and War* at Jack Tilton | Anna Kustera Gallery, New York, summer 2001.

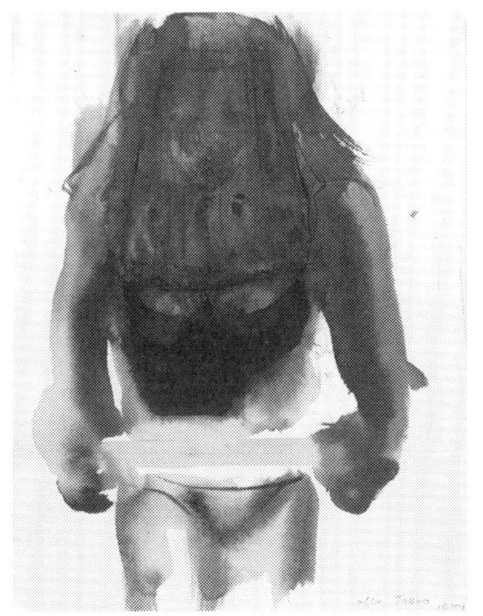

After Taboo 2001 45 x 45 cm

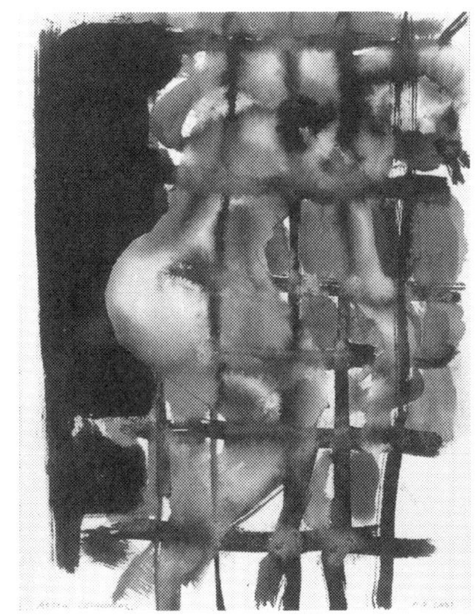

After Chathedral 2001 45 x 45 cm

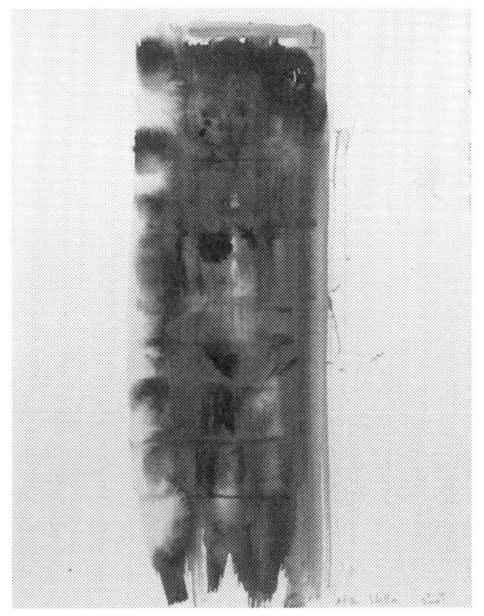

After Stella 2001 45 x 45 cm

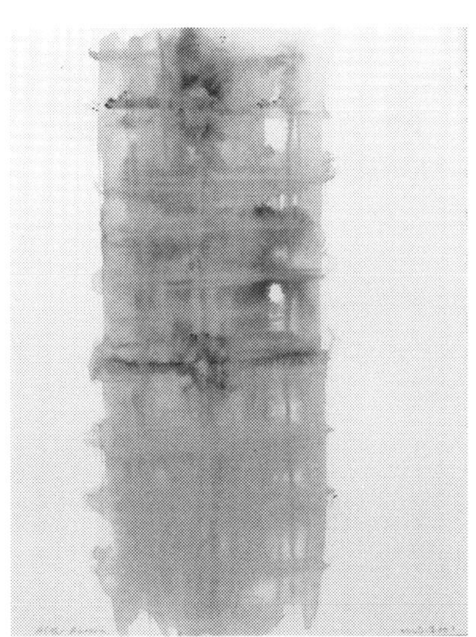

After Aurora 2001 45 x 45 cm

Wake-up Call

Or, from the talk to the walk,
from the studio to the exhibition,
from the dark room to the bright lights,
the day after the night before.
The worst thing about an exhibition is
that not everyone is in it.
The best thing about an exhibition is
that not everyone is in it.
The moral of the story is
that art is not about equality but about discrimination.
The tragedy of the story is,
whether you are a good or a bad artist,
there will always be someone who hates you.

You know you are a Foreigner

You know you are a foreigner
when you don't want to go home.

You know you are a foreigner
when everyone says the country you come from is beautiful to *visit*.

You know you are a foreigner
when you talk about the socio-political role of the artist and your tutor tells you, you'd better decide if you want to be Florence Nightingale, Joseph Beuys or an artist.

You know you are a foreigner
when you start to defend *here* what you have always criticized *there*.

You know you are a foreigner
when a show is called *Morning Glory* and you do not associate the title with a flower.

Suspect

Looking at images does not lead us to the truth,
it leads us into temptation.

It's not that a medium dies.
It's that all media have become suspect.
It's not the artists' subject matter that's under fire,
but their motivation that's on trial.
Now that we know that images can mean whatever,
whoever wants them to mean, we don't trust anybody anymore,
especially ourselves.

The Girls' Room
I am not a visionary
I am not a witness
I am just afraid.

The Lovers' Room
If you can't see it, paint it.

The Drawing Room
We are not God(s). Everything we draw,
we draw after (the fact).
A dead image is never as dead as a dead person.

Simplicity

It is very simple.
Eros is about coming
and death
about going
somewhere.

About Heaven

If death
is a womb
then heaven
is a body without fear
that invites one
to enter from
whatever side
one pleases
and just for a while
time doesn't matter.

There is one death
but there are many heavens.

The Right to be Silent
A Conversation on Elitism and Accessibility

'For whom do you make your work'? he asked me. 'I have the right to know'.

That humans have so many rights, does not make a silent painting wrong.
I don't do it for the people and I don't do it against the people.
If at all, I'll do it from the people and after the people. I never use the word 'elite'.
I don't gatecrash par ties to which I'm not invited. Everyone should not go everywhere. Making things easy doesn't make them better, but making things unnecessarily complicated, that's evil too. Being hard to get is all right, only if there's something to get. Heaven has always been quite an exclusive place, preserved only for those that come from certain clubs, not classes though. Believers understand that to get to a high place, you have to suffer and answer riddles and expose spies and marry the wrong person, and speak in tongues, so as not to end up in a low place like hell. You have no right to get in. You have to beg, pray and get down on your knees to get access to that place: to cross that border.

'But what do you think your work means'? he said. 'You seem to use populist images and have elitist intentions'.

There's what I mean and what you mean and what the work means or rather as Mr. Eco says, 'there are the rights of the text and the rights of the interpreters and the rights of the interpreters has been overstressed.' So between my (frequently irrelevant) intention and your (mostly veiled) intention, there's the intention of the artwork.
But if the artwork remains too silent, then I'll just have to refer you back to my statement from 1993:
'They say you can't judge a book by its cover.
You can't judge a woman by her lover.
But paintings have to be judged by their covers and their lovers'.

The Death of the Author

'I don't want to see your source material', he said. 'It's of no consequence to me when I look at your painting. It is no excuse and not part of the material evidence of the final work. You can't judge a painting by the picture that inspired it.'

It started with a black and white photograph in a Dutch newspaper of 14th March 1986. Céline was photographed in his bed, his deathbed, 1st June 1961. The article reviewed some books written about his life. I love to read old newspapers.
There is a face covered with a white sheet.
There is a face cut off by a white sheet, covering the nostrils and mouth.
There's half a face like an egg, the top part of the egg showing.
There's geometry of tragedy at work.
The sheet, like a Malevich rectangle, comes from the outside. The skull is bending, pulled down by gravity, while the lower eye, like a vertical cut through the face, mediates between the two parts.

'Most people want you to tell them everything you can remember about the making of an artwork. I hate people telling me their dreams', he said.

Serrano made a photograph in a morgue, of a man with a sheet covering half of his face. I've never been in a morgue. My father died at home. We looked after him. I did not look at him after his death or rather we did not exhibit him after he died, for a last public farewell. My mother slept that night in their bedroom while the corpse of my father was not removed yet. She said that while he was alive I was not afraid of him, so why should I be now, that he's dead. He took a long time to die. I was 12 years old and the doctor said his illness made his skin color change very rapidly. Once, about 15 years later, I tried to make a painting of him. It was a lousy painting. I didn't know how to approach the matter. That was an instance of being deliberately vague. It was an indecisive work. It had nothing to do with ambiguity. It was just unclear.

'One can't speak for the dead', he said.

The South African writer Antje Krog said that the philosopher Derrida came to Cape Town and said, concerning the truth and reconciliation trials, that one could not forgive the unforgiveable and one could not forgive in the name of the dead. And Krog's African colleague said – 'I can, because I'm in contact with the dead, they speak to me and are with me. Thus why may I not speak for them'?

Immaculate

'I'm not moved', he said. 'It's too static'.

It's so sad, I said. As if no one ever entered here. As if no one ever returned from there. As if it has never been used, as if all colour has gone from the inside, has been drained. This is not the origin of the world. This is the end of the world.

I'd like my paintings to be very bare.
To be as minimal as a figurative work could possibly be, without being dead.
With the image forever resisting the physical limitations of its frame, its material conditions as a painted thing: the paleness of the skin with the black-nippled corners.

'The playing at the edges gives it scale.
Without the edges it would be nothing', he said.

If a painting needs a wall to which it can object, an image needs edges to which it can belong. She brings no news. The only secret she hides, is that you don't love me anymore. But why should I burden you with that? Maybe it's better to look at her without trying to get to the First Cause. Cause then we're back to square one. Is this what we call inaccessible?

There've been times when I invited you.
There've been times when I confronted you.
There've been times, but not this time.

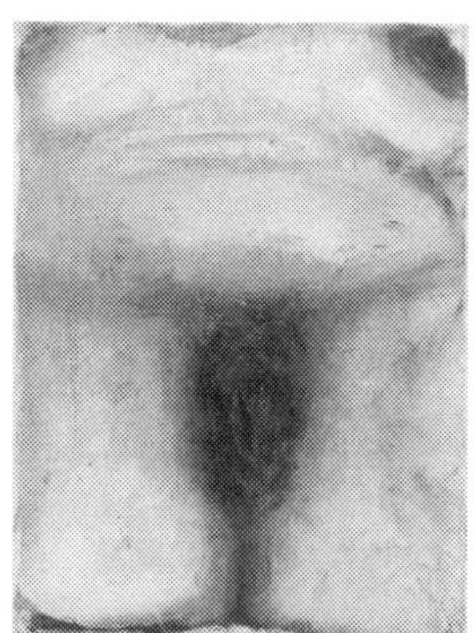

Immaculate 2003 24 x 18 cm

The Second Coming

If we get to heaven
and meet the Big Bright Light,
what will it be,
the eyes of the saints
or the flash of the camera?

Pretty Boys

Once upon a time, you didn't exist
when I came here, to Holland (thirty years ago).
You didn't yet exist here then
(your fathers did, but they were different).
You didn't exist yet,
as 'The Moroccan',
as a specific group,
as a concept,
as a subject, as a picture,
for every newspaper, TV and magazine column
(I was not an 'allochtoon' yet and neither were you).
But when you came
so did the attraction and the fear.
You, the Mediterranean type,
the physiognomy of the Latin lover,
the Arab on the white scooter,
the lover boy, the rapper, the Palestinian brother…
And the Dutch daughters fell in love.
And their fathers grew confused.
And called all Turks Moroccans
(all Moroccans are named Mohammed, Rashid or Ali,
all the Dutch boys are named Piet or Jan).
Her new Turkish boyfriend said
'your father and I have at least
one thing in common:
neither of us likes
Moroccans.'

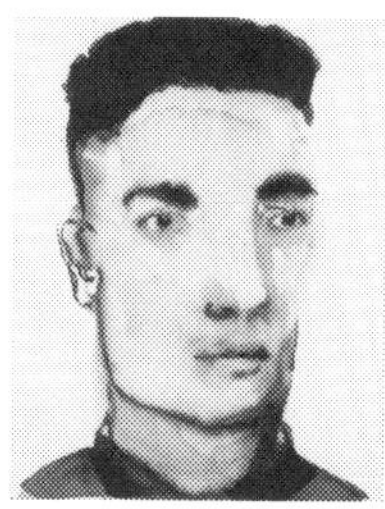

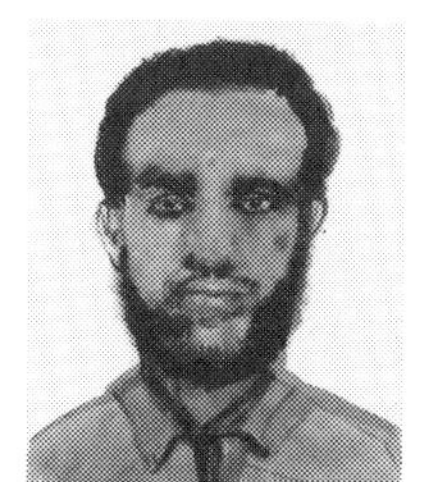

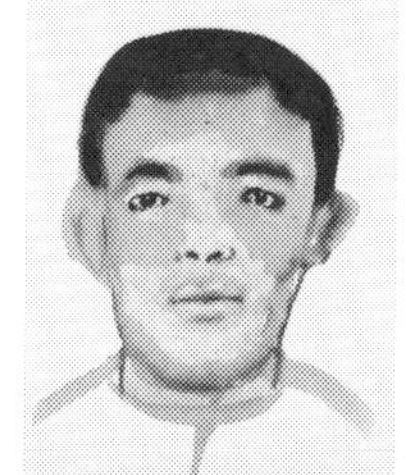

Young Man 2002–2005 (3x)45 x 35 cm

Man Kind
(or here's to those who inspired me)

This is not the times
for The Family of Man's smiles.
We travel in disguise,
so how would you know
friend from foe?

The devil is back, as two-faced
and as polarizing as ever.
Who's side you are on
depends on where you're from.

But for those of us who like Edward Said,
the tension between
the first names and last,
determines what comes to pass.

Here is to the popular culture
of image suppliers,
the embedded journalists, the media managers,
the hotel warriors and the airport artists.

Here's to portraiture, more or less,
used by politicians, martyrs, murderers,
the military... be my guest.

Here's to the skull of Charlotte Corday
who assasinated Marat, quite calmly they say,
and faced the guillotine without rage
at twenty four years of age.

Here's to the posters that Ad van Denderen
photographed in the region of the West Bank.
Here's to the Israeli soldiers who refuse to fight
in the occupied territories.

Here's to Amos Oz who spoke about the fact
that Jews and the Arabs are both
former victims of the same oppressor.
This makes their conflict harder not easier.
They have both been humiliated,
discriminated against and persecuted by
European Civilization.

Here's to the guys that took a trip from Birmingham
to Pakistan and then on to Afganistan, but met the USA,
and ended up in Gauntanamo Bay.

Here's to the actors of Shouf Shouf Habibi.
Here's to the boys in the streets of Amsterdam.
Here's to the difference between forgetting and forgiving.
Here's to the distinctions between, freedom, fate
and destiny.

Here's to where we start and where we go from there.
Here's to the fact that life is round
and what comes around
stays around.
And for better or worse
we are part of the same kind.

And God Said – I told you so

God saw that art was all alone,
so he put him to sleep and gave him kitsch.

Or maybe, kitsch started with the fall from grace,
with the first denial, with the first stupid lie,
the first cover-up after Adam and Eve had
eaten from the tree of knowledge of good and evil.
When they started to look for ways to hide their nakedness.
When Adam, with tears in his eyes, looked up to the
Heavens and said 'she did it'.

And God said 'Get out of here, couldn't
you think of something more original!'

So off they went, out beyond the gates,
to colonize the West and all the rest.
But just as they started to enjoy dancing around
the golden calves, God struck again in all
His eternal wisdom and amoral jealousy
and gave them the no-image commandment.

Deuteronomy 5 verses 7, 8 and 9
'Thou shalt have none other gods before me.
Thou shalt not make thee any graven image
or any likeness of anything that is in
heaven above, or that is in the earth beneath
or that is in the waters beneath the earth:
thou shalt not bow down thyself unto them or serve them:
for I the Lord your God am a jealous God,
visiting the iniquity of the fathers upon the children,
unto the third and fourth generation…'[1]

And there for us (the children of Abraham, the
Father of Christians, Muslims and Jews)
the image problem started. Don't blame the
modernists, they just rediscovered our old
mystic, abstract roots. They didn't mean to make
it difficult, they just wanted to make it simple.

The catholic Jesus, tried to appease God by saying,
'Father forgive them for they know not what they do',
but then Jesus never painted a picture or wrote a book.
His fans did.

I was always concerned about what God would want me to do.
I always wondered if art was good enough for God, and if so
what subject matter would be worth pursuing. I knew sexy was low,
erotic a bit higher and sorrow the noblest[2].

Now in 2006 we know that all subjects are equally low,
or rather as Freud paraphrased Goethe, 'The highest and the lowest
are always closest to each other in the sphere of sexuality.'
I'd add, the same goes for politics, too.

Give God a break. Let's talk politics.
Kitsch started as a German word, they say.
Although I could have sworn it was an American invention
or something that they used to make in China.
But we shouldn't blame the Germans for kitsch.
The third Reich put one off kitsch, but also off art.
When it came to paintings they liked kitsch,
but when it came to music, they liked art.
In the South Africa of Apartheid (pre 1994)
politicians didn't care about art but also didn't
even know that kitsch existed. They just censored
anything that moved.

Kitsch is not pink,
if you want to give it a color, make it white
(repeat, all the good reasons for no equal rights).
If you want to racialise it, give it a hood.
If you want to give it a sexual preference
don't make it gay.
I know the Taliban is not o.k.
but no one should have to look at
the National Geographic all day.

Kitsch happened when we discovered that we
could imitate and reproduce, whatever we want,

without having to believe in it; without having to cry or die for it; we can represent anything without paying for it, emotionally, intellectually or spiritually, because others have, or will, pay for it.

Gerard Reve said 'Free love does not exist.' Celine 'You don't do anything for free'. You've got to pay. A story you make up, that isn't worth anything. The only story that counts is the one you pay for. When it's paid for, then you've got the right to transform it.

1 Holy Bible, The Gideons 1961, u.s.a.

2 *A true Hedonist is hard to find*, *MD-light*, 1999

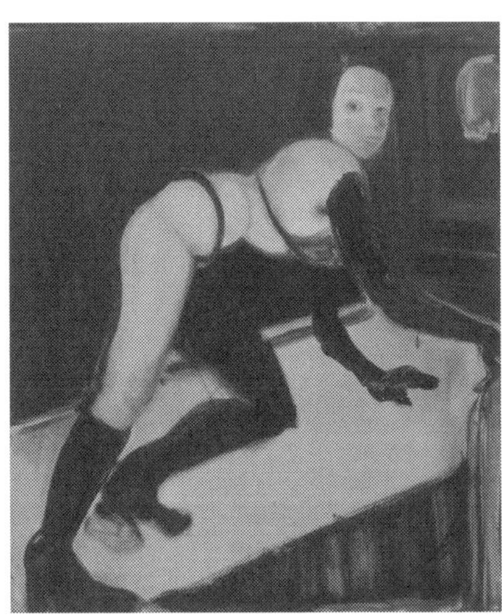

Adult Entertainment 2000 130 x 110 cm

On Photography and modern Life

Whether you start with a photographic source or not, that doesn't change the basic assumption that a (modern) painter is more interested in images that in the actual living of modern life; and that painters are more interested in images than in the actual living of modern life; and that painters are more interested in their own intentions than in their subject matter. When Picasso told Brassaï that photography had liberated painting from the subject, he meant it in a positive way, but this could also be understood in a negative way – one could say that painting is also free from the responsibility of caring for and about its subjects. We can paint anything without asking the permission of – or negotiating with – the original subject that has been photographed, because our 'model' – that is, all photography – has become public property. We do not have to be where the scene is taking place. But this is part of the tension of a good artwork, that one cares and at the same time, one does not really care…

Even though it seems to be the amateurs that take the most dangerous and important historical pictures these days with their mobile equipment, painters can remind us of the fact that while there is no progress in art like the 'old' moderns believed, that's no reason not to portray the never-ending cross dressing and makeovers, the camouflaged ways in which history repeats itself in our own time.

Adult Entertainment or what do I do
(when you are far away)

What do I do when I use a picture of a (wo)man
that I do not love, do not know
and have no interest in getting to know in real life.
Why do I use source material from porno-books as
models for my figures,
if it's not the pornographic that I'm after?
Because I can't see myself when I do the things I do,
I don't know how I look when I look at you.

Hommage to the Polaroid

The only camera I ever liked and ever used
was the Polaroid camera.
The Polaroid, always and only, true to its
own sublime distorted nature.
Fast and fickle and hands-on physical,
not concerned with digital vanity.
Cheap and expensive at the same time.
No copy and no negative.

p.s. Without you, no *Jewish Girl*,
no *Pregnant Image*,
no *Occult Revival*, no *Jule-die Vrou*.

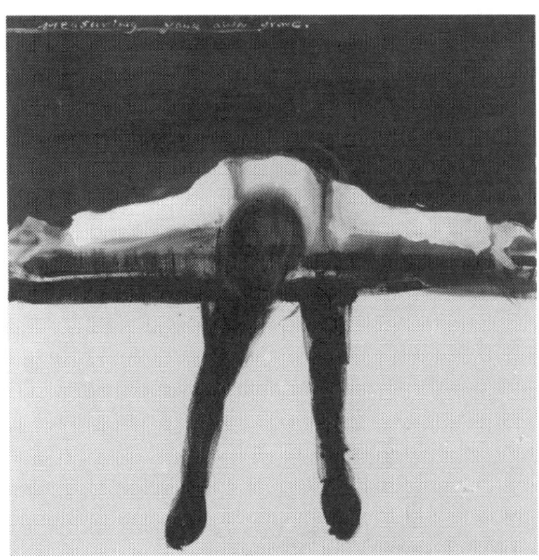

Measuring your own Grave 2003 140 x 140 cm

Measuring your own Grave

I am the woman who does not know
where she wants to be buried anymore.
When I was small, I wanted a big angel on my grave
with wings like in a Caravaggio painting.
Later I found that too pompous,
so I thought I'd rather have a cross.
Then I thought, a tree.
I am the woman who does not know
if I want to be buried anymore.
If no one goes to graveyards anymore.
If you won't visit me there no more,
I might as well have my ashes in a jam-jar,
and be more mobile.
But let's get back to my exhibition here.
I've been told that people want to know,
why such a somber title for a show?
Is it about artists and their midlife careers,
or is it about women's after fifties' fears?
No, let me make this clear:
it is the best definition I can find
for what an artist does when making art.
And how a figure in a painting makes its mark.
For the type of portraitist like me,
this is as wide as I can see.

Framing and Naming

Naming (a work) is important.
Framing (a work) is crucial.

I wanted to make many beautiful new works for my USA show
but in the end, I only painted a portrait of Marilyn Monroe.
The Monroe that died.

During the McCarthy hearings in 1954, Marilyn Monroe was threatened. If she did not get Arthur Miller to frame his colleagues, she would never be heard of again.

In her last interview in Life Magazine (1962) she said:
'Once I was supposed to be finished, that was the end of me.
When Mr. Miller was on trial for contempt of Congress,
he was told that either he named names and I got him
to name names or I was finished. I said "I'm proud of my
husband's position. And I stand behind him all the way"'.

I never wanted to paint symbols.
I also never wanted a painting to be a symbol.
Jean Paul Sartre said it was out of cowardism
that we fell into the symbolic.
I've said, I paint because I am afraid
to be dead while still alive.

Southern Comfort

There's always been a lot of water in the sea.
Now there's too many Chinese in Africa, maybe.
And what about the Americans in the Congo
who were undercover, without telling me?

Left the white beaches of South Africa
for the dark continent of Europe and now
the United States of America.

Never knew that Columbus went the wrong way
looking for a shortcut to get to the East, to China.
Instead he stumbled upon America
and realizing that it was somewhere else,
he thought, this must be India!
So that's why he called the natives Indians.
In 1620, the Mayflower brought the first group
of pale-faced pilgrims to America.
In 1619, a Dutchman brought the first group
of African slaves to America.
Centuries later, in the late 1960's, I was sitting in Africa
reading *Time Magazine* and listening to Janis Joplin
singing Big Mama Thornton's song, *Ball and Chain*.

North Africa (Woman of Algiers)

Home of the striptease.
Home of the dance of the seven veils.
Home of the ancestors of Abraham,
forefather of the Jews, Muslims, and the Christians.
Home of a God that does not want to be reproduced.
About Algiers, Nelson Mandela had military training there,
learned lessons of guerilla tactics from their liberation war.
Delacroix made a painting called *The Women of Algiers* (1834),
women relaxing in a peaceful female harem.
In 1954, Picasso made (one of many) sensuous paintings
inspired by this French-African source.
Little did he know where this orientalism would later go.
In 2000 I saw a photograph of a young girl standing naked,
held by - 'exhibited' between - two posing French soldiers.
It was taken in 1960 in Algiers.
I painted my *Woman of Algiers* in 2001.

Beaches ain't what they used to be.
(The Tourist meets the Fugitives)

As the newspapers inform us
daily immigrants are washed ashore
on the coast of Southern Spain.
Illegal African immigrants trying to get to Europe,
dead bodies on the beach,
Arriving in the promised land.
Bystanders trying to reanimate a body
on a beach in Southern Sicily.
The European Union is worried.
The Italian Minister of Reform said
'After the third warning, just shoot.
Otherwise, this is a problem of which
we will never get rid off.'

Expiring Dates

There are as many
different important dates
as there are different
wars and love stories.
Take 9/11.

11 September 1922
The British government promised European Zionists
a homeland for Jews in Palestine.

11 September 1990
George Bush Sr. declared war against Iraq.

11 September 2001
Hijacked jetliners hit the World Trade Center in New York,
destroying the Twin Towers.

12 September 1977
Steve Biko died in South African police custody.

12 September 2007
My mother died after noon.

Don't mention the war [1] John Cleese

The Third World War

Or, how 'Post-War art' has become a contradiction in terms.
We have to stop the Second World War so we can stop the Third World War.

Or, how the language of the Second World War blocks the vision on the present war(s).

The Middle East conflict will not be solved if one keeps on calling it a choice of being either 'for' or 'against' Jews. Supporting Palestinian rights is not the same as claiming that the Holocaust did not exist. Being against the policy of the Israeli government and the occupation does not make one an anti-semite. In Michael Sorkin's book *Against the Wall*[2], both Israeli and Palestinian voices contribute to the critique of the 'security fence' from a variety of perspectives, architectual, legal, historical and philosophical.

The Jewish Susan Sontag said in her speech on *Courage and Resistance*[3] 'Here is what I believe to be a truthful description of a state of affairs that has taken me many years of uncertainty, ignorance and anguish to acknowledge... The decision of successive Israeli governements to retain control over the West Bank and Gaza, thereby denying their Palestinian neighbors a state of their own, is a catastrophe – moral, human and political – for both peoples.'

The Jewish Noam Chomsky in a discussion at Fort Collins in 1990[4], replied to those believing that the Palestinians aren't really suffering but are people that advertise their misery and that they are only doing it for the cam ras because they are trying to discredit the Jews: 'They do exactly the same thing when there are no cameras.'

There are cultural differences in expressing emotions and the Western world tends to be less explicit. I think of our cold funerals where women with fancy dark glasses try not to cry, as if it was in bad taste to spoil their make-up. A Jewish Dutch student[5] dismissed the photographs of dead children in Gaza as Islamic propaganda and he called it, Pallywood.

From the horrors of reality to the fiction of images. One of the Jewish actors in the movie *Inglourious Basterds* by Quentin Tarantino[6] called the movie 'kosher porn'... Thinking of 'revenge' as a legitimate dream, the film reminded me of the catalogue of the show *Mirroring Evil; Nazi Imagery in Recent Art* at the Jewish Museum in New York[7]. Focussing on the perpertrators rather than the victims, it included Piotr Uklanski's work *Untitled (The Nazis)* [8], compiled of 116 photographs of movie stars in Nazi roles. Without the clarifying text the possibility of attracting Neo-Nazi's is always present.

Which reminds me of the fact that every image needs a text to protect it ...

and every text needs someone to de-code it

1 John Cleese, in *The Germans, Fawlty Towers*, 1975.
2 Michael Sorkin (ed), *Against the Wall. Israel's Barrier to Peace*, 2005.
3 Susan Sontag held her speech *Of Courage and Resistance*, at the Rothko Chapel in Houston, March 30, 2003.
4 Noam Chomsky, *Understanding Power: The Indispensible Chomsky*, J.Schoeffel and R.Mitchell (ed), 2002.
5 *De Volkskrant*, 17 January 2009.
6 *Inglourious Basterds*, Quentin Tarantino, 2009.
7 Cat. *Mirroring Evil; Nazi Imagery in Recent Art*, N.L. Kleebatt (ed), Jewish Museum New York, 2002.
8 Piotr Uklanski, *Untitled (The Nazis)*, photographic series, 1998.

Contra o Muro

The first mark is the worst.
The drawing of a line cuts the paper in two.
The drawing of maps and borders turns neighbours into foreigners.
Within military cultures whole generations of children have grown up, thinking only in enemy-images.

Art is a way of sleeping with the enemy.

I have enormous respect for the photojournalists who risk their lives in order to show us what is happening in the here and now.
I am not trying to improve their work. I am not a direct witness.
I am a studio artist. I travel in my imagination, or should it be,
I 'live' in my imagination.

I don't want Israel to be destroyed.
I want the occupation of Palestine to end.
I want us to stop the Second World War,
so we can stop the Third World War.
But that cannot be painted. Walls can be painted.

For me painting never felt like a window or a mirror of the world.
Maybe I see it more like a door with a NO ENTRY sign,
or a letter with 'Return to Sender – Address Unknown' written on it.
Or a checkpoint.

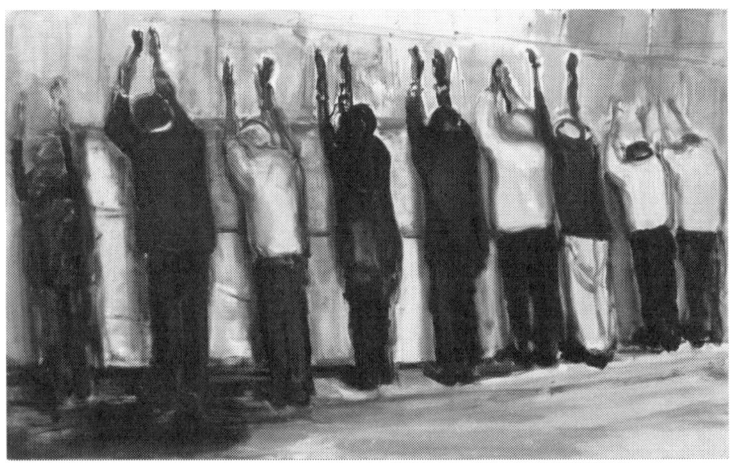

Wall Weeping 2009 180 x 300 cm

Against the Wall. Letter to David

I've been trying to write to you about 'the why' of my paintings,
write it clearly so that it is not only my sentimental story, but something
that is similar to a public statement. But the more I try, the more I get
tangled up in places I don't want to go.

Is it because the rhetoric of South African apartheid feeds my distrust of definitions and at the same time my longing for them? The naming of things and people. The spirit of the Law against the letter of the Law. The artist as some stuttering Moses having heard the commanding voice from the bramble bush. Here I go back to the Bible for my metaphors again. The first book in my life, teaching me that love and fear goes hand in hand.Everything that is important enough to move me, stirs these simultaneous emotions.

I often open books at random to see if there's a message for me. Still do.
Now too.

I read the Bible therefore I paint Against the Wall.
I read therefore I paint?
It's been said that Protestants read the Bible and Catholics look
at the pictures.

At this stage of my life, I paint the pictures and then I read the books.
The images come first, then the thoughts.
I 'fall' from the one wall to the other, from one type of arms into another.
First out of context and then into context.
From belief into disbelief.
But the more I understand, the less I can speak.

Thinking about religion, I always saw Christianity as a Jewish sect.
Only in recent years did I hear that some Christians blamed the Jews for killing Christ. Always understood that the Romans killed him (crucifixion didn't exist in Jewish Law or executions on Fridays). Never understood why it was important who killed him, as he was supposed to die for everyone's sins, and also didn't stay dead but was resurrected.

Dead or alive you have to go through the Bible to get to Palestine.

Against the Wall. Letter to David

The works on the wall

How are these paintings different from my previous works and how are they still the same? Always was interested in how things that look the same can be very different and vice versa. In a sense they are my first landscape paintings, or should I say 'territory paintings'. That is why they are so big.

For once it is not zoomed – in vertical frontal heads and naked figures that take the main stage – but a man-made architectural structure in a more perspectival narrative space. It leads us not into a holy land, but rather to a barren no-man's land.

I never liked architecture. Never thought I would bother to ever paint concrete slabs! Never wanted or could draw mechanical straight lines. As a person, but also as the type of painter I am, I was often very unhappy working on them.

It seems I have taken my own sentence – a painting needs a wall to object to – literally.

Two of a kind

First there is the body language, then the story.
I was a young woman when I painted *Dead Man* in 1988
with his Christ-like posture.

I was an anxious mother with a teenage daughter when I painted his 'partner' *Dead Girl* in 2002, using painting as a prayer for protection.

Only much later I read about the connection of these two young hijackers with Palestine and the German Autumn of 1977.

For Whom the Bell tolls

My exhibition *Mankind* showed how every age produces it's own 'Most Wanted' faces[1]. The emphasis of this show was on male suspects.

In 2007 my mother died at noon at the age of 86.
For Whom the *Bell Tolls* was about loss and departure, but also about transformation and freedom[2]. A spirit set free, my grief and her relief. So I made the (film) stars and the gods weep for her.

As a child I was fascinated by portraits of (female) film stars. A movie star can love, cry and die and then get up and do it all over again, each time in a different time and place and with a different lover, staying desirable yet distant forever. They can play both victim and persecutor.

It also paid hommage to *Hiroshima mon amour*[3], a most touching example of the modern cinema's ability to portray the intimacy of a (fictional) love affair, the (documentary) tragedies of politics, and simultaneously expose the language of film and time itself.

1 *Mankind*, solo exhibition, Paul Andriesse Gallery, Amsterdam, 2006.

2 For *Whom the Bell Tolls*, solo exhibition, Zeno X Gallery, Antwerp, 2008.

3 *Hiroshima mon amour*, Alain Resnais, 1959.

A gothic Story. The final Tale.

Once upon a time, there was a film star and a painter who wanted to change places. The painter wanted to be a star, so make-believe, so multifaceted, but still approachable. And the star wanted to be a painter, deep, authentic, blissfully independent and wise enough to know that there's something bigger than mortality. The painter thought the star was sweet but naïve.

The painter told the star that one painting was not necessarily art, that today it's all about exhibitions and an exhibition is more than just a collection of paintings. Paintings don't speak for themselves anymore. They acquire meaning from their context, the labels attached to them and the touch of the exhibition curator.

The painter told the star that curators have taken over the art world and that amateurs have superseded photographers, especially when it's about the here and now. They no longer want to produce photographs that look like paintings, but to capture the revolution digitally as fast as they can. To speed up the Spring. Get the news out as soon as it happens. But the more powerful and influential a medium, the greater is its potential for distortion and lies. A painting of something does not prove that it actually happened (a photo still can). It would never be accepted as evidence in a court of law because by its very nature it cannot be a true representation of reality.

That's the root of the nagging, eternal problem of subject-matter. Oh, how terrible! Everything must be shown, but not everything can be shown. If God does not exist, he cannot be portrayed. But if he does exist, he may not be portrayed. Art is incomprehensible? Life is incomprehensible. There's a constant clash between the senses, between nonsense, senselessness and sensuality. That's why a good work of art is essentially elusive. It is not out of arrogance that artists don't want to 'explain' their work (as for me, just ask and I'll go on forever). Silence is sometimes the better answer.

'What about sexuality?' the film star asked. In painting even the Nude isn't what it used to be, not with the kind of relationship that artists and models have today. Not that Hollywood has ever known how to deal with it. They're especiallywary when it comes to male nudity, as if there would be no more war if we got a glimpse of a man's sex. To say nothing of the Egyptians who in 2010 called for a ban on the *Tales of a Thousand and One Nights*. Every culture imposes its own censorship. No wonder art and culture are two different concepts. Art delivers us from the constraints of our culture. It is almost as hard to find an erotic work of art in a pornographic society as it is in a fundamentalist culture.

The painter was getting into the swing of it. The film star's attention began to wander. The painter said, 'There is so much more that people don't talk about. It's also important to have *the right name*. How far would Malcolm Little have got, if he hadn't changed his name?' 'Malcom who?' asked the film star. 'Malcolm X', the painter replied.

But are we talking about fame now or *colour*? Painting is colour conscious, but racism implies taking a political stand, and we want to avoid that, don't we? When a black art student suggested putting a self-portrait on his invitation card, his teacher asked, 'Can't you find something more neutral?' So rather than spoil the atmosphere by pursuing the matter of taste and colour, they turned the conversation to the demise of painting. The assassin comes in different guises. Now it's the market, they say. But their talk was interrupted by the sudden appearance of a dark figure dressed all in black, who said that painting *could* not die because it belonged to the realm of the non-dead. Painting is too ancient, too primitive and too pleasurable to disappear. Its patron is Count Dracula, whose reflection doesn't appear in a mirror, nor his image in a photograph. He stayed only briefly and flew off before daybreak.

I am not here to defend painting. That is done by every painting that stands the test of time and by every new generation of artists. In our image laden culture, painting has grown accustomed to not being the star of the show, but takes its place in a far larger constellation of visual brilliance and garbage. To those who argue that art is elitist, I would say that every game has its own rules. Take football, if you must. To begin with, anyone at all can play. But not everyone turns out to be an Ibrahim Afellay. Every discipline has its particular challenges. I know that people get frustrated because art keeps striving to change its rules or expand its horizon. That is precisely what makes it difficult and special, and what makes it different from a hobby. If we can learn anything from art, it is that we cannot claim to stand for freedom of expression if we cannot tolerate differences, however disturbing they may be.

Royal Awards: Queens, Stars and Painters

First, I want to say it is gratifying that the Royal Awards were introduced to promote young independent painters, and that they are still presented today. The event itself is nothing sensational. It is held in a palace, that much is true, but the presentation – two works by each of the winners – on short, display walls cannot be said to have any real impact on the space. Nevertheless, it is moving. The challenge of constraint, the power of a small but compelling gesture.

The South Africa that I come from has never been a monarchy. It was colonized first by the Dutch, later by the British. My mother protested by refusing to rise to her feet for the British national anthem. In London in the late 1970s Johnny Rotten of The Sex Pistols sang his punk version of the song *God save the Queen, she ain't no human being.*

But Holland is not England. In the Netherlands of 2011, our Queen Beatrix is wiser and more tolerant than the present cabinet of ministers. They applaud and support internationalism in the arts, but not a multicultural society at home. Art, however, has always been poly, not mono as far as other cultures are concerned – Van Gogh moved to France, Alma Tadema, born in Dronrijp, was knighted in England, Mondrian and De Kooning went to America.

When I was young, I thought that queens existed only in fairytales and Walt Disney films and that princesses died out after Henry VIII and the French Revolution. My big worry was that all those beautiful ball gowns would disappear along with them. Fortunately, we were spared that calamity. Fashion comes, fashion goes, not that painters today do much with clothing. But what would dreamland America and celluloid heaven Hollywood be like without their Oscar Awards? That reminds me – from princesses to presidents – of another iconic moment in American history: the sensual, hear breaking shots of Marilyn Monroe singing 'Happy Birthday, Mr President' for JF Kennedy in 1962, just months before she died. Has there ever been a painting as poignant? Maybe Rembrandt's tragic Lucretias losing their honour and taking their life, are among the most beautiful paintings I know. They are less well known in the Netherlands, probably because they are in American collections and rarely travel.

Is there still a place anywhere that paintings can truly belong, for everyone to see? Museums are no longer safe havens. I know there's too much of everything, but it's nice to preserve something of our vanity for future generations. Recently, in 2008, Jeff Koons became the first modern artist to exhibit his work in Versailles. He felt at home in the splendid extravagance of Louis XIV's palace. He said 'We are contemporaries'.

Europe was synonymous with painting until the 1950s, when New York took the lead, and for years afterwards America was all that mattered. No one was really interested in non-Western art, but in the 1990s the former colonies started to take their sweet revenge and make their presence felt. Europe began to feel old, then tired, then threatened. But this is not the time to complain, for there is much to be done. The flatter the world becomes, the more obvious it is that painting is still necessary.

Every Prize has its Price

The Beginning is the hardest

The end merely follows. In the beginning is the end, with art as well as with speeches. Where and how do you begin?

Maybe I should start with the most difficult bit and after that we can party. First I want to explain all the reasons why I should not be standing here and all the reasons why I am standing here.

Actually I've been busy with these two questions all my life – why am I here and should I be here? A writer once said (I forget who) 'We are here to better the lives of others', but why the others are here we really don't know. (Funny that when one paints portraits, people automatically assume that you like people, but 'it ain't necessarily so'!) In our home in South Africa we had a *Mad Magazine* type-text on the wall, 'I Love Mankind – it's People I can't stand'. Ok then, but we can't do without each other. It is our duty to relate to each other, whatever the cost.

I've been given a state prize but I'm not sure I understand what a state means – the word 'state' is used so often in conjunction with 'international terrorism' that I begin to feel we are living in a permanent state of war… A good friend reacted 'Marlene, a state prize! It is time to run!'

About the Character of Prizes and Role Models

In 1964, Jean Paul Sartre was the same age as I am now, fifty nine, when he refused the Nobel Prize for literature. He said he didn't want to become an institution and that it would affect his freedom. Susan Sontag accepted the Jerusalem Prize for literature in 2001, but not without unease as was evident from her acceptance speech (available on the internet).

Every honour has its cons and every prize its price.

Actually I came to the Netherlands because of a prize. I received the Jules Kramer Scholarship from the University of Cape Town in 1976, providing two years study overseas. My mother said, when I threw the pebble against her window pane that evening to tell her I had received the scholarship, she knew I would leave. I didn't realize it myself then. It wasn't my intention to stay in Holland, although it was wonderful to walk the streets alone at night and read all the banned books. Holland was very good to me. I will always appreciate that. Holland gave me a place where I was able to take my distance. In 1976 TV reached South Africa for the first time and in 1983 I made my first appearance on Dutch TV. I thought the show was about the beauty of diversity, but there was a subtext, as the real focus of the program addressed the feelings of discontent amongst the Dutch about foreign artists taking advantage of the social benefit system.

From Foreigners to Allochtonen

'Ik is een alachtoon', I once made a T-shirt with this text (consciously misspelt). One might think I did it for the allochtonen, but that ain't true, just as I am not doing it for the autochtonen (another ugly word …)[1]. As I once wrote in an article about elitism: 'I don't do it for the people and I don't do it against the people, if at all I do it from the people'. Then there is the fact that I am a woman. I believe that art is androgynous but I am continually asked how it feels to make art as a woman. I could say I do it for women, but as my mother said to me, a month before she died, you certainly don't have to do it for me!

A Plea for the Arts

I accept the prize, because I want to make a plea for art. Art is not a case of innocent taste. A neutral gaze does not exist. Art is there to liberate us from the tyranny of our culture (Lionel Trilling), note, our *own* culture, not from the outside but the inside.

Art is there to remind us, that all laws about what is beautiful and valuable, were made by humans and can be changed by them.

I make the strongest possible plea, that the proposed legislation that has been put before the state, which would result in the elimination of almost all art education in our high schools, should not go through. It would result in the loss of the most important subject to survive in the 21st century. We cannot allow the Netherlands to become a country stuck in narrow cultural nationalism. We live in a global intercultural world. We send our youthful militants to Afghanistan but don't want to learn about their culture.

I suggest an 'inburgeringscursus' (a course for immigrants who seek permanent residence) on art and culture, for all future legislators who will be in a position to decide on the arts.

I propose that art evaluation will not be allowed to drown in market fundamentalism. I believe as the artist Hans Haacke once said, that the advertising giant Saatchi once said, that the philosopher Marx once said, 'Everything is related to everything else'… but sometimes I think… blessed are they, who have been spared the frenzy of the auction houses.

I propose that the Dutch take more pride in what is being achieved in the visual arts in their country. Take the quality of the post-academic institutions. The model that the artist's initiative, Ateliers '63, created in 1963, has had a positive influence on all contemporary post academic institutions and made them world-famous. Only the ministry of Culture, Education and Science does not seem to know this.

It is ironic and tragic that while the trendsetters call 'Small the new Big', the Ateliers does not get rewarded for these same principles – for which they've always fought – but instead, punished, with a zero subsidy. Support them out of pride, if nothing else!

I want to thank the jury for the honour, and for entrusting me with such a large amount of money, based on their faith in my insight in the arts. Also I want to stress that regarding art – you can't honor the top if you don't value the basis.

The beauty of art is that it teaches you to enjoy the freedom of the 'other'. (In that sense art is and was always in essence multicultural). But the difficulty is – that as an artist you are also aware that maybe you could have done it differently. Van Gogh once wrote 'I make art to give something back to life', I am grateful that I am able and capable of making this decision, that I will share with you now. Just don't scrap this prize (also not after 2016). It is a young prize, it wants to grow old too.

I accept the honour and give the prize money to De Ateliers.

1 In The Netherlands the word autochtoon is used to refer to the original inhabitants of the country, allochtoon indicates people coming from elsewhere.

An Artwork of the 19th Century that was and stays important to me. Even Fairies can be ok.

At the art academy where I started to teach in Holland in the 80s, there was a girl who painted fairies and witches. I agreed with the other teachers that this was bad, even as kitsch! Yet I, nor anyone else, could explain to the student what in essence, was the problem with her work. In the end all the different explanations seemed to come down to the same conclusion, that with this kind of subject matter it was impossible to make a painting. If this was true, it would imply that by definition certain subject matter was unpaintable. This bothered me extremely, but I lacked evidence to prove my point. Then I discovered a tradition not mentioned in my art history books and only found in Britain in the 19th century, a speciality of Victorian Times: the Fairy Painters! The father of Sherlock Holmes did it, a few others did it, but the one who really did it for me was Richard Dadd. Years later my excitement about my discovery had cooled off a bit and I had to admit that almost none of these fairy paintings would make it to my list of top 100 artworks. Except for one. *The Fairy Feller's Master-Stroke* by Richard Dadd[1] is a fantastic painting on all levels. It is wonderfully composed, layered, intense, intricate, complicated, decorative, elegant and mean. The moral of the story is: the problem is not the subject matter.

1 *The Fairy Feller's Master Stroke* (1855–64), Richard Dadd, oil on canvas, 54 x 39,4 cm

Non-traditional Relationships

Modern art is by its very nature a non-traditional activity.
Or rather it aims to expand our notions of the traditional and the normal.
Art is there to help us to see more and not less.
Laws are there to help us to love more and not less.
Laws should protect us from hatred and not from love.

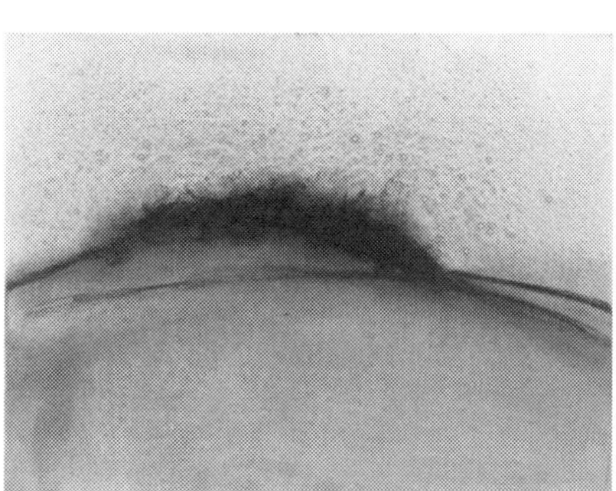

Magnetic Fields (for Margaux Hemingway) 2008 30 x 40 cm

Politics (of Art) 1989 – 1997

From one dirty Place to Another
As an art-student in the early 70's in (South) Africa, I discovered the problem of art and Politics. It did not result in more effective artworks, only in more people ending up at psychiatrists. As a postgraduate in the late 70's in (Dutch) Europe I discovered the politics of Art. That resulted in me ending up with a gallery.

Of a cold blooded Nature

A good gallery is an unfriendly place.

Unlike the warm, dark cinema where the self can dissolve surrounded by its own species, the gallery is a cold place, structured to increase selfconsiousness. One is more than ever aware of the fact that it is as an artviewer and artmaker that you are looking at art, trying hard to make (or avoid making) value judgements. Even if a gallery excels in enthousiastic welcomes, the artworks, having left the studio (or other production spaces) seem to soon catch a cold and show a drop in body temperature.

Touch of Class

The gallery is not a space.

The gallery is a personality.

The artist cannot be held responsible for everything the gallerist does or says.

To be a good gallerist you have to like art more than people, while being a good artist doesn't mean you have to like people, or art.

Showing and selling

I don't like to sell without showing. To be able to exhibit regularly at the same place is a privilege.

Unwanted Advances

The gallery has to keep people away from me.

Too many people and institutions assume things about the artist which they have no right to do.

The gallery should function as a protective barrier.

Artists of this Gallery

The only common ground I could find was that they are all still into the pleasures of the flesh and the touch of the hand.

Paul Th. Andriesse

When it comes to longterm relationships, I feel more at home with the manic depressives than the hysterical artscouts.

To be continued.

The Art of Exhibiting

It is not 'the imaginary' we need
neither is it 'the museum' we desire.

1.An imaginative exhibition is fine (creativity needs dreaming). An *Exposition imaginaire* is wishful thinking. Those who live too much in their imagination get run over by reality.

2.There can be no failure in the realm of the imaginary. That is probably why the Netherlands Office for Fine Arts, like many other authoritarian structures, can view their own activities with such illusions of succes and self-satisfaction. They decide on their shows, not through concrete dialogues with artists, but by preconceptions and conceptual self-deceptions.

3.The museum has lost its aura. Some galleries are more important than most museums.

4.The museum is losing its authority. Reproductions turn meaning into an ambivalent free for all. The question revolves around attempts to control meaning. Artists cannot deny this power struggle. To quote Barbara Kruger: 'We won't play nature to your culture'.

5.The elitist nature (by choice) of this meeting and discusssion shows that artists have not gained their rightful places when 'the art of exhibiting' is at stake.

6.When I say 'artists' I mean artists in general, but in case of Holland I especially refer to the Dutch artist who often still believes (just like 'the authorities') that an artist should be seen and not be heard.

My Thoughts on big Shows

It's not possible to participate
in Big Shows
without feeling this urge
to bite
the hand that feeds you.

Give me a face instead of a place
I don't understand Kassel (as a place)
it's too grey, too cold and too
far away for me.

Give me
the head of
John the Baptist.

Bacon and Dumas
– or the Discomfort of being 'coupled' –

The problem with me
and liking somebody,
is that it takes me so long
to acknowledge it publicly
that when I eventually do
it's mostly no more true.

All artists (have to) participate in GROUPSHOWS,
knowingly or not. Being part of any collection,
and/or art history, the art is constantly placed
in relation to other artists, mostly of their own generation
or those with the so-called same style and concerns.

I've been grouped
I've been solo,
but I've never been 'coupled'
in an exhibition.

I don't really *like* 'couples' (which doesn't mean I don't paint them). It is an inevitable part of culture. I believe relationships exist between everything, yet some are more extreme than others. Some attract one another against all odds, and some are more forced. Bacon would definitely, if he had a choice, have said no to this show (as Marlborough does)[1], because he would not have liked to be seen in relation to me. He wanted to compare himself as an artist only in relation to the very best (Velazquez and Michelangelo). I compare myself to whatever comes in my way. As Jan Andriesse said: 'The difference between you and him is: Bacon has a discriminating taste, while you don't discriminate'.

Is this then a *forced* relationship? Not really. This was not initiated by me or him, but *arranged* by others. Yet saying yes to this, made me feel (initially) like I was trying to seduce or make unwanted advances to the Pope, moved by the aphrodisiac of his authority. But then at the same time: Which woman of our time wants to be associated with the Pope at the end of the 20th century?! I had mixed feelings (as usual).

Bacon, just like Picasso, is an artist that deserves a bit of a rest after his death. Both of them, each in his own way, got so type-cast by the media and public opinion, that one forgets what they've really achieved. Picasso simply became Mr. Macho, and Bacon Mr. Horror. (I once made a joke on myself by calling an exhibition of mine Miss Interpreted, note – *not* Miss Misinterpreted, but most people missed the point, just causing more misrepresentation).

Anyway, I got caught between my earlier youthful admiration for Bacon and the image he had become. I even felt a bit embarrassed, then for him, then for myself. Yet I don't know of anyone of the generation after the Second World War who ever wanted to paint a portrait of a human figure (whatever their intentions) who could escape Francis Bacon. Dutch artist Emo Verkerk mentioned that he started his first drawings after being inspired by that (now famous and classic) interview of Sylvester with Bacon.

1 Marlborough Gallery, London, takes care of the estate of Francis Bacon

Reasons to Say No (In Order of Importance)

He's a dead master.
He's a painter's painter.
He's got colour (but just one race).
He never drew.
He started as an interior designer.
He's English, no, Irish.
He was lucidly articulate (even though 'only a painter').
He's good.

He doesn't really use titles.
He still believes, however pulled apart,
in the raw power of the image.
He wants movement.
As Jolie van Leeuwen said: 'It is as if Bacon is creating works for the silent cinema and Dumas is making stills for films with soundtracks'.
His figures go through all kinds of motion inside the names of their frame.
Distortion becomes his means.
He wants to go directly to the nervous system.
He is searching for the essence of the human condition.
He shows the scream.
He had said: 'What do you imagine that an audience would want?
I have nobody to excite except myself.'

Reasons to Say Yes (In Random Order)

In the end I couldn't resist the temptation. As Bacon has said: 'An artist shouldn't called a fallen woman'. Bacon and Dumas have been accused of different but simi cinema, photographs and the cruelty of life. Our dependence on chance. And t sensationalist subject matter. And last but not least, there's the question of sexuali

She's a mid-career artist (sounds like midlife crisis).
She's not even a proper painter (just a type of part-time neo-conceptualist).
She's muddy (but concerned with the colour of the skin).
She draws constantly (though never as a sketch for a painting).
She knows nothing about design.
She's Afrikaans.
She radiates 'much heat but no light'.
She's 'worse than mediocre,
with only her titles sometimes worth remembering'.
She'll cheat and steal for a good title.
She relies heavily on the word.
She wants a sentence.
Hers are static.

Style collaboration (montage-like) is her way.
She uses sidesteps and backdoors.
She's searching for the perfect lover.
She shows the sigh.
She has said: 'Give the people what they want'.

Some remarks are quotes from published criticism

raid of making a fool of himself.' As I say: 'A female shouldn't be afraid of being
imes. There is his nihilism and my indifference. There's our interest in Picasso,
cusation that we've both been trafficing in images of misery, gothic horror and
likes men and so do I.

Deadlines and Airmiles

(or – The first time I flew in an aeroplane
I thought everyone had a parachute under
their seat, in case of emergencies.
I'm still upset that it ain't so.)

If I'm too late
for your deadline dates
for 'Transit'
it's because I've been in transit
for too long.

I've been on airports doing my
drinking-whisky-goodbye-rituals
too often
cultivating my feelings of multiple
personalities and double spying.

Indulging in romantic medieval thoughts
of chivalrous departures,
flying is such a sad suffering
for the sake of noble causes.
While my friend Jan calls it
much more abrupt
'Fucking up your mind
and fucking up the ozone.'
I take the taxi to my room and phone
to say I'm safe and to hear if all is well
where I am not.
And than I'm too tired to read, too tired to
reflect, too tired to think, too tired to see
and then I go and install my work in
whatever the place is called, where art is
being placed, for other travellers to see.

International Biennales

When Socrates made his plea *against rhetoric* and *for dialogue*, it seems at least some of the conditions then + there where a bit easier than here + now. For example, everyone at least used the same language codes. (but then again – he did still end up having to drink poison...!)

Now, we need good translators to make us feel at home, not only in the places we pass through or exhibite, but also where we live. Yet for artists this should be exciting times. The artist was always supposed to be a bit of an alien, now almost everybody is. So we're all in the same boat (or should I say port).

That is why I believe that international biennales are so important, when taking into account and working within these changes, it's a challenge for everyone concerned and permit me to say this: as someone who has participated in quite a few (better and worse ones) in my day, that it is good for young artists. Not to make them famous, but to make them see and experience how artificial this 'thing' called culture is. One has to test ones theories through practice, and check every now and then if your 'country' still exists.

Failing alone is not the same as failing together. Or rather as Sartre said: 'The hatred of others shows me my own objectivity.' In private you feel as if you are the subject of everything. That's why isolation and segregation (why not call it apartheid) is very bad for most artists. Among others you realise your objectivity. You realise your interrelatedness and/or dependence, whether you like it or not. You realise that culture is not just this sweet, warm, noble thing, but a constant ongoing struggle between people. Never mind if you call them the same or the other.

The 7 Year Itch
Many things have happened in these seven years since I've last written. We have lost some of our friends and artists. Some got damaged beyond repair, some left and some came back. We've turned grey and established. Like a Beckett play it goes. We can't go on. We go on.

From one Place to too many Places
As an artist in my 40's, having by now shown in many places and having collaborated with many different people, I don't know what I want anymore. I don't know why to say yes and why to say no. There is much to be said for loyalty, but how much loyalty can one woman bear. Now I don't only have my home gallery to worry about, but also all the one night stands. But then, everyone needs a hand to chew on.

Fresh Blood
A good gallery is a gallery that knows when to change. I've been told that the traditional cinema theatre is dying, getting lighter and lighter (leaving its black box). Let's hope the galleries dim the lights of their white containers and go darker.

Cheap Thrills and the Mid-life Crisis
The gallery is closer to Magdalena than to Maria. I always wanted a gallerist that dressed like a pimp. I always wanted to be a cheap artist and a rich woman. What went wrong?

Showing and selling
You know you're in trouble when you've moved from privilege to duty and from pleasure to pressure.

Protection
I don't like that word anymore.

Artists of the Gallery (see the 7 Year Itch)

Paul Verhoeven (Home? Don't mention that emotion).
I found out that I had something in common with the man who made *Basic Instinct* and *Total Recall.* When asked what he feared most, he said – psychoses. When the familiar becomes strange.

A united Europe

I never meant to stay
I suppose that's what they all say.

It was my first time in a peepshow
so when the girl smiled at me
I said 'Only looking' and she replied
'That's how I got started here too'.

Do the right Thing

Skeletons in the Closet

To write about South African art and it's politics (with the emphasis on politics) I find very difficult. I distrust myself and all others involved with all our multi-motivational defences and references.

Everytime I try, I shift my perspective and doubt my own sincerity. I want to say that the best art there is, is often of an amoral (not immoral) nature and that what's wrong with South African art in general, is it's moralistic attitude. And yet... what am I but a closet moralist myself. I can't stand all this tedious art theoretical terminology used in the artworld. We use it as a clever lawyer, to prove ourselves not guilty, while we know that words are useless when one happens to be at the wrong (or right) place at the wrong time.

Okwui Enwezor stirred the emotions of many by his essay, but it was not so much his articulated criticism that held the attention, but his use of the 'R' word that did it. Not response, not representation, but racist.

White People

don't move too quickly to grey areas. Racism is (still) present tense history (all continents included). White people share a collective guilt that will not be forgiven in our lifetime. No matter how often we say we're sorry, how long we study the past, read and quote the right books, what our individual deeds are. This is our fate. This is the black and white of it.

Identity

I only use that word when forced to. This is where that horrible apartheid concept 'identity' got us. Now everyone is using and abusing it. And how the artworld of the 90's love that term! After discovering the body (as if it was ever gone) they then immediately started to look for it's ID card.

Good People

In the artworld there are no hard-core racists left. The majority are conscious, clever and caring artists that make art that is described as being a critique of, or an investigation, or an analysis of something or other. That's not such a bad thing. Artists who are only interested in themselves are terrible bores; although those only interested in others are too good to be true. But then goodness as a personality trait has nothing to do with good art anyway.

Bad Deals

It is often very difficult for artists to distinguish between their intentions, their methods and the actual work that moves from their private world into the public world. We (most artist) use cliche's and appropriate images to some degree or another. There's nothing like an old cheap trick that works. Yet it's hard to be against a cliche by using a cliche. (It's healthier to embrace that which you use.) But one should not be surprised that at least some viewers will find it offensive and/or regressive or that those indifferent to racial references, will find it visually boring and thus bad art.

It's hard to be against degrading images and yet use it, and not get some perverse pleasure out of it. But if one wants everyone to join in the fun – then don't use images of those (long) dead or the anonymous, rather use images of those who have the power to sue you (as they should) if they don't agree with what you've done with their images.

Catch 22

Acknowledging and embracing ambiguity does not place one above suspicion. (That even stereotypes aren't one-dimensional doesn't simplify issues.) Trapping your viewers to expose their own prejudices reflects in many directions. As an artist, I don't display the explicit suffering of others and I believe I treat all colours as equally strange. Yet I've been accused (in reviews) of 'trafficing in misery' (in America) of being a 'rehashing of a Benneton ad' (in England) and even as 'a white person specialising in painting Black people'; because I often make dark works of figures of indetermined or non-specific origin; the ordinary white critic seems to perceive and thus describe everything that's not *very white* as Black.

The final Solution

Very evil people often make very sweet unconfrontational artworks. Look at Hitler's pictures. One could not deduce the ideology of that man from looking at his watercolors. (The nazi's collectively did love kitsch, tragedy and the sentimental.) After the holocaust most European painters did not want to portray human beings anymore. Especially healthy ones or the dead. The first out of disgust for the nazi's pure race ideology, and the other out of respect for the dead and shame that you survived, while they died.

More recently (the American artist) Rober Gober exhibited his 'sleeping white man and hanging black man' wallpaper in Philadelphia. But even though the black guard could accept that the artist didn't 'mean it' badly and that Gober wasn't a racist, the work was still unacceptable to him because in that whole museum this was the only representation of a black person, and once again, it was a degrading one.

Representation

This brings us at last to Okwui Enwezor's real complaint. He never said that artist could only represent those very much like themselves. He objected to certain types of representation e.g. representing the black subject repeatedly at the 'liminal point of his defeat', or as a source of reassuring harmless entertainment or in a too nostalgic fashion.

I BELIEVE NOBODY SHOULD BE REPRESENTED IN THIS WAY.

But then I don't like to represent anybody anyway (artistically speaking). I prefer to refer and to suggest rather than to capture and to re-create.

The moral of the story is not that artists shouldn't do what they feel they have to do but, as God says, do what you wanna do and pay for it.

p.s. No Woman no cry

A last word to the artists who happen to be women among us. Come on girls, let's face it, we can't look good all the time!

On Others 1986 – 2014

Erik Andriesse

Nightmares of Beauty

Once upon a time there lived a boy called Erik Andriesse, who distinguished himself from the passionless people around him by glowing in the dark. Now the country in which he lived was quite dark. Artists however, would talk about the extraordinary light in that country.

During the 1980's all artists were interested in the artificiality of life. A picture of a flower was much more interesting than the flower itself. Very few people still believed that everything that existed was part of nature itself. People lived in cities. Artists lived in their studios. Places filled with books, bottles and talk about art and artists and what was relevant and what was not. And they forgot to love... But Erik was aware of the fire that was eating his heart, while the clock ticked at night: the shortage of time, the repetitive movements of desire and the energy of the body watched by death. Flowers larger than life, dreams larger than life. Nightmares of beauty.

He was ignored by the calculators, whose blood did not rise when they saw his exotic death-dances on paper but he continued in his own impatient way. Erik is not a conceptual artist. Erik is not an associative artist. He is not interested in displaying the cultural-historical aspects of his subject matter. But Erik is also not the naturalist he seems to be. He even shows similarities (at times) to Spiderman, the comic-strip hero. Erik is not a cultural barbarian or a primitive. He reflects on the good, the bad and the ugly of the art world and the synthetic problems of painting.

As a friend said, 'Only to the extent that the paint neither disguises itself nor fades into oblivion, is it possible for the illusion of the flower to sustain itself. So we remain with the splendid contradiction that whilst the paint joyfully goes about its business of being a sunflower, simultaneously it never lets you out of its sight'.

To him, to skulls, to life, I'll drink a toast. To his eternal youth!

Lidwien van de Ven

The Body Guard

Dressed in Exposure

Time of the day – just before the night falls
Time of the year – always in the past
Identity – untitled
Sphere – autistic
Sex – female
Intentions – unclear
Dress – informal to naked

The Uncomfortable Audience

The impact of Lidwien van de Ven's work relies to a large extent on discomfort. She manages to make her viewer feel uneasy. Her audience consists mainly of those who blush or those who get angry. Those moved by her exposures interpret them as vulnerable in the extreme, while those irritated and distrustful of her appearances interpret them as one-dimensional, begging for attention.

But what does she want? She states, 'My work is about being there, about being and not having, about being able to and not about wishing to.'

Beggars on the street try to 'force' sympathy. They play on our collective feelings of guilt. Their expressions of need often annoy rather than melt the hearts they mean to reach. Does Lidwien use similar tactics? Or is it just those big eyes of hers that are 'too' big? What about similarities to animals that try to avoid punishment? The 'guilty' animal rolls over on its back or curls up in a foetal position, while pleading with its eyes. Instinctively it knows what to do. Aggressive behaviour is meant for the enemy and not for the master.

Lidwien's images do not display sorrow, shame or suffering. There is no objective reason to assume that we are dealing with guilt or sins committed. The viewers who read these images as accusations or apologies confuse their real-life relationships with women (or other half-naked beings) with Lidwien's portraits.

This brings us to the core of the matter, the amount of the sexuality on display. The 'Kill Rushdie' Islamic audience will have no doubt that this is the image of the Western Woman displaying her whorishness (never mind the art context). Such clear-cut explanations do have their charm, especially since most art criticism exhausts one with arguments that show how art always contains the opposite of what it seems to display.

Yet seeing that I believe art (by definition) cannot carry straightforward messages, being an interaction of the real and the imaginary, I dismiss this argument as oversimplification. On the other hand, this work must not be de-sexualized to make it easier to handle, or to ward off 'unlawful' thoughts.

This is an art that embraces sexual identity. The artist is both the subject and the object in these works. By her exposures we are 'forced' to reflect on our own notions of sexuality in art and life. Because of this, Lidwien does not make you forget your own limitations. She does not want you to identify with her.

She is somebody else. She is not your magic mirror. She remains a separate identity. She is not just 'the other' in relation to someone of the opposite sex. She is part of the 'otherness' of things that is, as she says, 'with us, but not of us.' Using one's own image in one's artworks is not necessarily narcissistic, just as selecting a pose, thus not being spontaneous, is not the same as faking. Her emphasis is not on the playing of roles but on the notion of selfhood, in spite of the fact that it might be impossible to show the self without becoming someone else. This brings me to a type of photograph which I want to relate to her work.

Females are insane (Portrayals of the Mentally Disturbed)

During the course of the nineteenth century, madness took on a female nature: woman = irrationality, silence, nature and body; man = reason, discourse, culture and mind (when men go mad it is because they have too many feminine qualities...).

Darwin's theories also contributed to the view of women as inferior (more primitive) beings. The internal nature was identified through the examination of the external nature. Photography – the new invention, praised for its objectivity – very soon became a useful tool for surveillance and control, especially in prisons and asylums that needed records to identify inmates.

In England, Dr H.W. Diamond (one of the pioneers of psychiatric photography and a friend of Lewis Carroll) 'modelled' many a mad woman on Shakespeare's Ophelia and other ruling aesthetic models of femininity of his time. A woman's appearance was very important. If she did not pay enough attention to her dress, it could be read as a sign of lunacy, but too much attention was easily seen as the malady of intense vanity.

Lidwien's images mostly have an unkempt or even a dirty appearance. The bodily positions she selects remind me of the dual expressions of mental illness as found in previous centuries, the tension of mania coupled with the passivity of melancholia. The melancholic is portrayed in a withdrawn self-enclosed manner (often with face obscured or hidden by the hands), next to the exposing pose of the maniac. Lidwien also places herself in environments of confinement - or rather isolation - that bring to mind the self-contained world of the insane.

I do not see these correlations as diagnostic signs with which to read Lidwien's mental state. I see them as expressive signs, consciously or unconsciously borrowed from the vocabulary employed in medical illustrations. It is these undercurrents that give her work its own special flavour: sex perfumed with the memory of madness.

Freud banished the depiction of the insane (he rejected the idea of 'seeing' the patient) from psychoanalysis. The introduction of abstraction in parallel with the introduction of psychoanalysis removed the actual representation of the insane from the fine arts. Now, at the end of the twentieth century, the body, with its discomforts and pleasures, is brought to the attention again.

I'll end with the case of Dr Charcot of the Paris clinic Salpêtrière, who had a photographic workshop installed in his hospital in 1880. There female hysteria was perpetually presented, represented and reproduced. The specialty of the house was hysteron-epilepsy and the star of the asylum was Augustine, also known by other names. For five years she was the example most frequently used for his studies. Then she got rebellious and violent, was locked up and escaped – disguised as a man. She was never found.

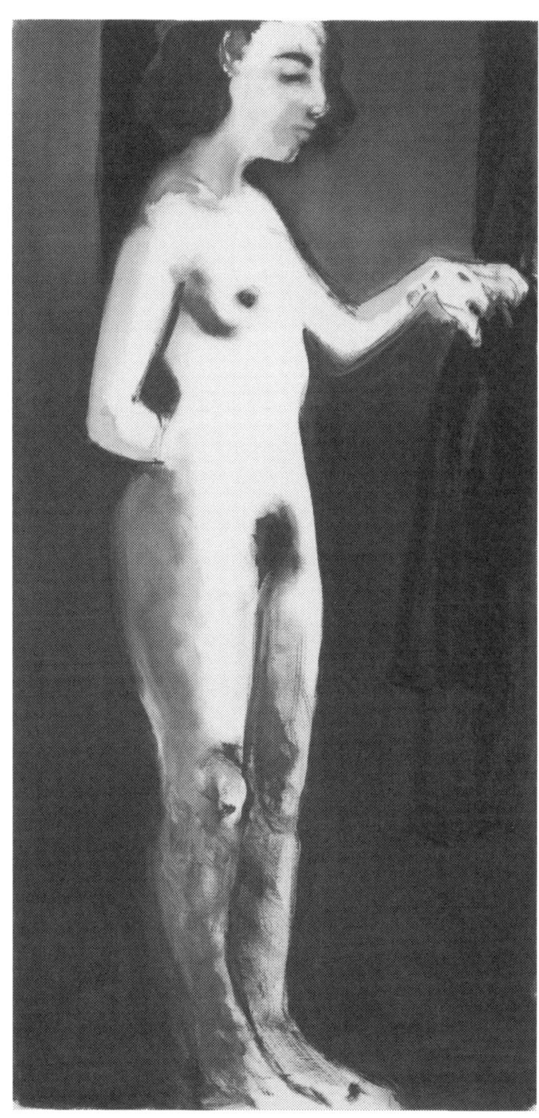

Missing Picasso 2013 175 x 87 cm

Jan Andriesse

The Tyranny of Reality and the Autonomy of Painting

The work of Jan Andriesse does not show the conflict from which it arises, nor does it play on the sentiments it houses. The construction is buried under layers of paint. Half in jest, but telling, is the following statement he once wrote;
To get you down, a list of painters' seven-up lethal sins

1. painterliness
2. pain
3. passion
4. pleasure
5. pantheism
6. panderism
7. purpose

At a time when art has become increasingly aware of its audience and tries not to alienate any of his viewers, his art is indifferent to either the seduction or the provocation of others.

His use of bleached tones is often mistaken for pastels, due to retinal laziness by those saddled with the popular notion that softness implies weakness.

These tones are the colours of dusk. The hour of the fall when light turns dark and non-colour sets in.
But his work is no rage against the dying of this light.
It is a state of submission. It is a slow process that cannot be manipulated but that has to be revealed.

Jan Andriesse

Future Perspective
or why he's not the Man they say he is

You may call him a superficial surface fanatic
(and you won't be far off)
but you can't call him a utopian fascist.
He never uses the words pure, ideal or perfection.
It's realism he's after.
It's the echo of nature,
not the man made illusions of heaven
that he seeks.

Since the sacred and the sublime
have been appropriated by the mediocre
and the modern is no more,
there's the kitsch of a sunset,
the pink of flamingos in the zoo,
the cheap thrills of make up,
the bleached blondes of the Albert Cuyp,
to rub against the golden section.

When his paintings work,
they embody this cosmetic-synthetic seductiveness.
They embrace without touching.

He might only wear white
but he's no monk.
He might love his ear-plugged silence
but he relishes the noise of a good mean argument.
He might be obsessed with the chain curve
(though it took him five years to hang one properly)
but he grudgingly admit,
that it will never beat the curves of a woman.

Anton Corbijn

Live Acts. Silent Studios

Now that it's over I want to start

It's hard for me to work next to and with someone whose work I like, not that it's not exciting. Although I work alone and with printed matter as my models, I've always been attracted to photographers who work with real people. But it doesn't seem to bring out the best in me. It's the same with live models (whatever their occupation). I worry about what they think of me and I get even more worried about what they think, I think of them. And then I lose the freedom of the amoral touch which for me is requisite for making good painting.

The naked Truth

The public display of nudity has always been one of my main artistic interests, as well as the reasons given to justify or banish it. The traditional (male) painter uses it to promote higher aesthetic values, the fashion model to promote clothes, the porn industry to promote masturbation, while film stars only do it if it's part of the story. Most people don't do it at all...
And the teaser makes you beg for it.

A Slow Hand

While in life teasing is experienced as a bad deal flirtation, leaving you angry and frustrated, as an art form it has given us the striptease.You enter the theatre of seduction. You pay for this pleasure of quivering with anticipation. You stick to the rules. Strippers might stretch rules, you don't.
You have to know your place.
You have to come, so that she can make you wait.
In our fast forward culture, they say that we've traded the tease for the strip, magic for illusion, glamour for humour.

Yet a really good strip is never fun(ny).
It's hard to find, but when you do, you don't laugh.
You shiver, a memory of ancient origin. Salomé's erotic dance drove the king to give her whatever she asked. When the seventh veil fell, after all was said and done, she asked for the head of John the Baptist: a Bible story showing the power of desire. Not love, but desire. Do Anton and I look at girls stripping in a similar manner? I am the sister and he is the son of a preacher man.

Strippinggirls

Neither he nor I choose to show dangerous dancing women intending to do you harm. He is even more kind in his manner (but then he's no woman). His gold framed peepshows are playful, not mean. He is used to working with people with professions and with clothes on. My painted figures of the imagination are mostly naked, without accessories or actions giving clues to what they do, have done or would do. With his project the opposite is true. Small differences make big problems for painters. The figures in most of my work don't even have feet to stand on so I had to paint boots and platform shoes to show that they are doing their job. They undress to be in control. They are more shy with their clothes on, than off.

Anton and I are both known for stripping people. We both do portraiture. If it is true, then it's not so much about exposing roles, or making the rich look dirty or the famous ordinary. It's a stripping down to that melancholy sex appeal that makes surnames disappear and first names fictional.

Frank Stella

Notes on All is Fair in Love and War

Thinking about Blocks, Bars, Crosses, Crossing out and Crossing over…
The Politics of Geometry versus The Geography of Politics

I've always enjoyed making links to other artists.
This often shows through my choice of titles,
which to me is like a child's game.
The similarities between these works are often
only cosmetic.
Take my 'Stella' and compare it to the early Frank Stella's
I so admire for their cool American beauty of (seemingly)
effortless clarity.
My Stella is a figure that can't decide whether to be solid matter of fact or just a figure of speech. A figure caught between a flat space and a deeper space – a hard, aloof space and an illusional emotional space. It is not about which is the better place to be.
It is not even about making a 'she' out of a 'he'.
It is just my way to pay my dues to all the different types of Stella's that have crossed my mind.

Vincent van Gogh

As good as it gets. Van Gogh is the one

Now that 'Obsession' is the name of a perfume and
Freud don't slip no more, we no longer have to make
Vincent too beautiful to be true.
Van Gogh was not Antoin Artaud.
Van Gogh was not the star in *Lust for Life*.
Van Gogh was not keen on insanity.
Madness caused his death, but not his paintings.
Many an artist has a tragic death, but not many had such a focused and intelligent pictorial mind. Many artists died poor, but not many worked so hard and thought so clearly.

'It is very probable that I shall have to suffer a great deal yet. And to tell the honest truth, this does not suit me at all, for under no circumstances do I long for a martyr's career. For I have always sought something different from heroism, which I do not have, which I certainly admire in others, but which, I tell you again, I consider neither my duty nor my ideal.'[1]

For him, art was a profession like any other profession. He did not place himself above or outside of time. He was constantly referring to and comparing himself to other artists, dead or alive.

'I think that art, the old fashioned idea of innate genius, inspiration, etc. – I do not say must be put aside – but thoroughly reconsidered, verified – and greatly modified.'

He was neither innocent nor primitive. He looked at nature to find models, because he did not want to 'invent' subject matter, just as one cannot 'invent' passion. For him, the radiating sun became a better model than the gloomy potato eaters. Joy served him better than sorrow.

'Joking apart, I am of the opinion that a man or a woman ought to be desperately in love with something or somebody, and the only precaution one might be able to take, is to do it in a certain way according to one's ideas, and not in any other way'.

Van Gogh did for portraiture what Manet did for flowers. Van Gogh may not have been the first to place the figure in an abstract space, but he knew how to electrify it better than anyone that came after him.
Van Gogh painted the artificial colours of the Polaroid before the Polaroid camera was invented.
Van Gogh painted 'glow in the dark' luminosity long before the disco nights.
Van Gogh invented acid green and sulphur yellow before anyone heard of chemical warfare.
Van Gogh said 'don't paint the wall behind the head, paint infinity', that is why Barnett Newman could get afraid of red, yellow and blue.

If advertising people are still looking for an image that sticks in your head, whatever your psychology or culture, Van Gogh had already created it.
If Frank Stella said he tried to keep the paint on the canvas as good as it was in the can, van Gogh did the same for the paint from the tube. That's as bright as it gets.
If Warhol can do it without doing it, so can Van Gogh.
He is not a painter of nudes or eroticized landscapes like his friend Gauguin, but he is a better lover.

1 *Vincent van Gogh, The Letters*, Jansen, Luijten, Baker (ed.), Van Gogh Museum | Huygens Institute | Mercatorfonds, 2009

Marijke van Warmerdam

Tomorrow

Marijke makes me look up
when I want to look down.
While I sleep with yesterday
she dances with tomorrow.

Caravaggio might paint no sky
but men do cry and wonder why,
the Divine made no sign
when Lucy lost her eyes.

Melissa Gordon

Collateral Damage
Or, Paintings of Pictures that show that a Painting isn't a Picture

Once upon a time, there was an American girl who came to Europe to further study her art. She worked for a while in a studio in Amsterdam, where before her, a Turkish-German girl had made paintings, in a building where an Irish guy almost made a film on Auschwitz, while a Jewish girl from Israel made a film about the Documenta with her Moroccan friend. The country where she came from is very proud that they saved the Dutch in the Second World War and got there before the Russians did. The USA is also very proud that it hasn't had a real war in its own country for a long time and it has managed that, for many years now, by being at war abroad instead. When your friends in Holland start talking about norms and values, you know the next stop is Afghanistan.

Melissa Gordon is the kind of artist who takes the bubbles out of the Coca Cola, who brings the White House into the White Cube. Her painting has an attitude. It's flat, but it throws a shadow. She has made a series of paintings that deal with the tradition of collection and re-appropriation of art and pompous images that the White House has collected, an idealized image of success, with titles like *Flag (Pomp and Circumstance)*, *Three Treaties (for the end of conflict)* and *The Winners*. (Marcel Duchamp called a title the invisible colour of an artwork).

As a woman of the world, she is not alone when it comes to being interested in image-power and its perversities. Luc Tuymans has also targeted the American way of life in

Proper, a recent show in New York. Melissa's mood is less grim, but no less tense. She gives women their due and one might also think of Michael Borremans, but unlike her he is a surrealist and although she often uses fragments of pictures alongside each other, she is also not a collagist like Neo Rauch. There, however cold the execution of the works, you end up facing a world of fantasy.

With Melissa, you 'enter' the painting. The painter knows that you are there, but'they' don't know that you are there. The paintings are self-aware, but we're lured into spaces where others are not aware that we're entering. In an Eric Fischl painting for example, you watch the boy watching his mother. You look at the woman undressing for the man. You look at Americans interacting, doing their daily business, public or private. You watch. They do. You judge. They act. With Melissa it's not like that.

In a Melissa painting, you are inside. Inside someone's head. Inside someone's house and you are not supposed to be there. You wonder if the bookcase is just a cover-up for a secret door. I spy, I spy with my little eye. You could be a detective looking for clues. You pick up the binoculars and see some-one with a gun. But this time it's not science fiction. And you are not the good guy trying to solve the crime. You are the killer who polishes his shoes every day and wouldn't hurt a fly. You are the double agent. You are the figure that one does not see in the paintings. You are the real subject of the work. You move your eyes up and down over the walls, the desks, the bulletin boards, over the floor of these frozen spaces. Everyone freeze – don't move! You are the woman who wrote the notes then; and now you are the one who has to decipher the handwriting. Who did it? The nurse, the doctor, the psychiatrist, the senator, or you: you with your split personality?

Keren Cytter

Improvise. Lalala and Halloo

<u>When I cry, do you want the tears to run all the way or shall I stop halfway down?</u> Child actress Margaret O'Brien

<u>They used to photograph Shirley Temple through gauze, they should photograph me through linoleum.</u> Actress Tallulah Bankhead

Where shall I start, knowing that where one starts is crucial to the meaning of a story, because the end is already there, determined by the beginning. How shall I start, in what way, knowing that the tone will color all the rest that follows. She said to me 'just improvise', so I thought, yes, let's do it as she does it. Improvisation is the key.

Once upon a time... My father was a farmer who liked to play the violin, although one of the strings was missing, he would accompany anyone's song, even if he did not know it. He would say 'I'll just improvise'. (Apart from that, his other favorite sayings were, 'you can fool some of the people some of the time but you can't fool all of the people all of the time' and 'never trust anyone, not even your own father').

I was born in South Africa in 1953. Keren in Tel Aviv in 1977. Maybe that is one of the reasons why we have sympathy for one another. We met in Amsterdam when she came to study there in 2003. I was (supposed to be) one of her tutors. Never really taught her anything. Never really thought she wanted to be taught. She was accepted at the institute because of her films, her writings, dialogues and scripts. Not really because of her drawings.

Did I like the work? Was it nice, like Warhol would use the word 'nice'? No it was not and she wasn't nice either. She was beautiful however, although she did not use that word much. As Diana Vreeland of Harpers Bazaar and Vogue said, 'There is no elegance without very good humour'. And yes Keren's got humour. Sophisticated as hell. She doesn't tell jokes. People who try to crack jokes all the time are not very attractive. It is not about laughter. It's not a 'hahaha' funny humour, nor a sour humour. It is a humour that understands the insult.

It is a cruelty that comes from a keen intelligence, mixed with an extreme emotional vulnerability and a cute awareness of one's own stupidity and inability to understand one another. And yet that's all we've got, We don't play the fool. We are fools, not clowns.

Laurence Olivier called Marilyn Monroe 'A professional amateur'. Keren is one too. She uses the artificial characteristics of her medium quite naturally. She is an "'and' and 'and'" girl supreme. She deconstructs, superimposes, leaves out, jumps, mixes, subtitles, in videos like television, like films, like movies, like soaps, like cinema, like theater... Like multi-layeredness was her middle name.

I even found some Fellini that made me think of her. Federico Fellini was talking about how he needs an elastic scenario, and how actors who learn their part by heart, made him feel uncomfortable. 'What if I want to change the text? What if a new scene comes to mind? What if I feel like improvising a completely different movie? Or taking up another profession?'

He watches his actors offscreen eating and talking about soccer or ordinary things. So, in the movie when the actor has to say, to his love or his son, 'Get out of this house', Fellini can say to him 'Please do it like the day you told the waiter "You have brought me overcooked rice". Indeed, I sometimes go as far as making the actor actually say "You have brought me overcooked rice", instead of "Get out of this house". Later on when dubbing you can always get that line back in.'[1] Maybe Keren would just leave the food sentence in there, in a manner of speaking, but it would probably be spagetti instead of rice.

Things keep on going wrong, yet they never totally collapse. Tragedy is postponed. When, before the deadline, Keren sent me the pictures of her drawings by email I ended up in a slight state of panic. Lets call it (con)fusion. Me not being so computer friendly yet and not being used to handling the world of digital information overflow, getting lost in abreviations and non-existent attachments. A world of blunt assumptions and messages. I couldn't find her messages. Our communication went somewhat like this.

Keren: 'Soon three strange emails will be sent...
The subject is lala. The subject is lalala. The subject is halloo'.
Many mails later I at last found what I should.
The titles of the drawings were: *Patttern of Violence 1 2 3; Chair; Vertigo; 2 Lobby Cards; Untitled; Ovgu; A Bag on the Floor Camouflaged.*
The titles were not: *Explore the Seven Wonders of the World Learn More; Get better answers from some who knows. Try it now; Get news entertainment and everything you care about in Live.com. Check it out.* (These were the hotmail texts that were on the same pages that I read as information relevant to Keren).

I found the images. Keren's drawings are terrible. They are drawn and colored in with a marker. Hard and 'insensitive' like the voices of her friends playing her actors, with unnecessary decorative patterning that reminds one of the impersonal drawings of the insane. *The Pattern of Violence* drawings remind me of the publicity line for the film made of the play *Who's afraid of Virginia Woolf*, 'You are cordially invited to George and Martha's for an evening of fun and games'... Her drawings do not please me. Because she does not want to please me, or you. That is what makes them so good.

1 Federico Fellini, *Faces*, 1981.

Jean Auguste Dominique Ingres

The portrait of Joséphine-Éléonore-Marie-Pauline de Galard de Brassac de Béarn, Princesse de Broglie

One of the most gripping exhibitions I have ever seen was the Jean Auguste Dominique Ingres (1780-1867) retrospective in Paris, a few years ago.

The most beautiful of the many halls was the one dedicated to his portraits of ladies dressed in the fashion of that time, with dresses just as emotionally expressive as their facial expressions. I singled out *The portrait of Joséphine-Éléonore-Marie-Pauline de Galard de Brassac de Béarn, Princesse de Broglie*, painted in 1853, precisely one hundred years before I was born. (This lady died aged 35, after her death her inconsolable husband kept the painting hidden behind a curtain). As is the case with all good portraits, not everyone agrees about what her expression means. According to her husband she was very religious and shy, he described her expression as one that reflected the perfection and purity of her moral character. But one critic characterized her expression as one of cold reserve and aristocratic contempt. It is true that Ingres' women usually appear very pensive, as if their thoughts are elsewhere, as if they are absent-minded. Clearly, they radiate more of Apollo's calmness than Dionysus' spontaneity. It is almost mask-like and so different from the equally masterful, but more intimate Vermeer's *Girl with a Pearl Earring*, who looks at her spectators with longing and full of desire. Josephine is far more aloof. Both paintings have blue and golden yellow as their most striking colours but where Vermeer's is gentle, warm and in soft focus, Ingres' focus is sharp.

And yet I also see in her expression, qualities which Goethe attributed to blue, a colour which seems to both sooth and stimulate. 'Just as we enjoy looking at a pleasant object, not because it urges us to, but because it attracts us.' It reminds me of the shiver when I felt attracted for the first time to a (still) unspoken love. In English 'blue' stands for both depressing and transcendent things, for melancholy, sacredness and pornography ('blue movies'). John Lee Hooker said that with the creation of men and women 'the blues began'.

Because of her immaculate satin dress with so much blue, I go on an imaginary journey, to the East and to Africa. I even find myself in heaven: blue as the colour of distant longing of which the realization lies far away. Westerners have

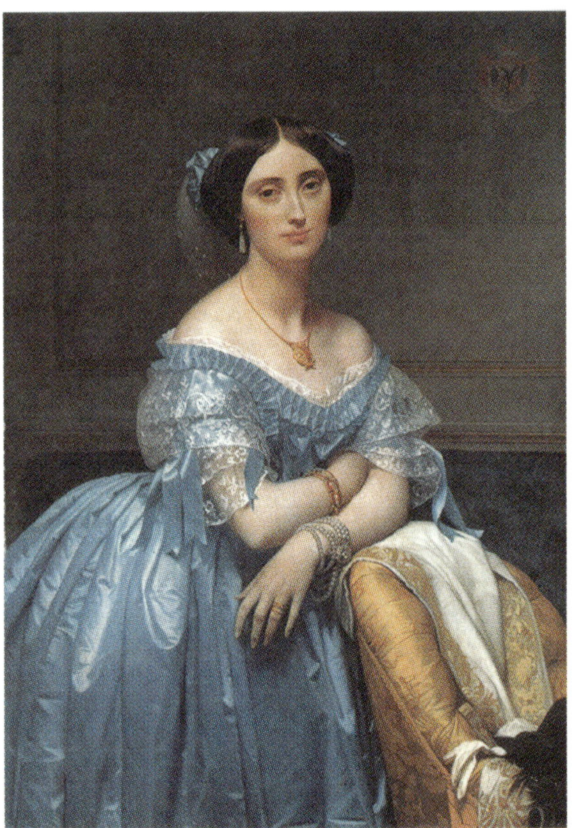

The Portrait of Joséphine-Élénore-Marie-Pauline de Galard de Brassac de Béarn, Princesse de Broglie 1853 121,3 x 90,8 cm

always wanted to go over the seas and later on, in the hereafter, to heaven. Blue also stands for going 'over the seas', going over the horizon. Once, ultra-marine blue was the most highly-priced pigment, bar gold. The medieval word oltramarino means 'over the seas'. It was not just used for blue but also stood for 'imported' goods. This is how the Virgin Mary, the most painted woman in Christian art, acquired her blue cloak from the East. This most valuable blue came from Afghanistan, the semi-precious stone lapis lazuli from the mountains.

It is not just in European symbolism that blue is the colour of heavenly powers. The skin of the Egyptian God Amur is of a blue colour which enabled him to fly through the sky unseen. The dancing Krishna with his blue skin becomes even more seductive due to his contrasting Indian yellow loincloth. Ingres' princess also makes use of the alliance between yellow and blue, and of Europe and Africa. Across the arm of her chair hangs a white, gold-embroidered cashmere cloak of North African origin, which became popular in Paris during the French occupation of Algeria. The chair is upholstered with gold-coloured silk. Hope is somehow heavenly. Usually the halos of angels are golden yellow and their wings are blue.

I once wrote the following about eros and death. 'It is so simple. Eros is about coming and death about going'. Ingres shows us the erotic domain, a sensual world of dazzling colours and flowing lines which is perceptible but inaccessible. You cannot take possession of what you see in a painting. You can only lose yourself in that which is not yours alone.

The painting shines due to a continuous intensity and concentration. Everything, every single detail, is equally important. The colours do not have a fixed identity. In fact, colour is the emission of energy and it is like everything in the universe: it trembles, vibrates and changes continuously and yet remains one. We keep forgetting this and that is why we are so afraid of death, until we stand before a work of art that radiates light. It gives me hope that death is perhaps not the most terrible thing that exists. This is not an idle, self-satisfied painting with an easy message of comfort. Ingres knows that it is impossible to paint a portrait of a woman (he said so himself). And this is the paradox, that he tackles this fearful realization with so much constant precision and love, without hope of reward.

Alice Neel

Alice doesn't live here anymore

When Alice Neel started to become better known in America in the early 1970's, I was an art student in South Africa. By that time, in my existential search for the human face and figure, I knew the work of Bacon and Hockney and looked at the photographs of Diana Arbus and the silk screens of Andy Warhol, but no-one showed me Alice Neel. However, when I did finally stumble on a reproduction of her work somewhere, it immediately stuck. Strangely, when I got to Holland in the late 70's, no one there knew about her either.

I never met Alice Neel in person. It was not because she was a woman or had a difficult life that I fell for her. It was not because of her witty writings that I was attracted to her work. I only discovered that to my surprise, much later on.

What struck me as very special, very welcome but truely extraordinary was the fact that not only did she paint ordinary people sitting on ordinary chairs who were actually dressed in the (by now outdated) colorful fashions of their time, but in spite of, or, at the same time, it was also still a modern painting. It was her achievement, that she could paint anxiety in bright (even decorative) colors. My generation was taught that modernism did not like the seasonal changes that were the natural realm of fashion, because art dealt with the universal, the timeless and the eternal. Art should not illustrate or be tied to the likenesses of a specific time and place. That is why, even now, I mostly paint naked people, because I still can't picture the sublime with a dress on.

Most figurative painters of the late 20th century placed their figures in a sort of nowhere or non-space. Alice always located her subjects. She lived somewhere. People live in a place, share the same space. They are related. There's been a lot of artistic talk about 'Identity' these last 20 years. Critics love the noun, placing the emphasis on the wrong spot. Alice used the verb. She identified. It is about identifying 'with': to find the right balance in the power struggle between the artist and subjects. That is the transformative magic of portraiture and Alice painted portraits. She didn't paint models, she didn't paint masters. She painted people.

Most figurative painting is not about people or rather they seldom paint 'characters'. Guston painted cartoons. Warhol public images, Chuck Close uses portraiture to paint about painting, Katz paints the cool, Peyton paints dreams...

It is interesting to note that in the recently published, *Art since 1900: Modernism, Antimodernism, Postmodernism*, by Foster, Krauss, Bois and Buchloch, the word 'portraiture' does not appear in their elaborate index, neither is there a mention of Katz, Close or Alice Neel for that matter[1]. They do mention somewhere the fact that conceptualists regarded the portrait as a historically obsolete model...

Neel is a modernist portrait painter, if you wish. When her paintings are good, they vibrate and tremble with an energy as nervous as Munch. It disturbs and disorientates without making use of extreme expressionisms or surreal proportions or dramatic distortions (coming from the African continent I don't call her akward perspectives 'distortions', it seems quite naturel to me). It's a mixture of Picasso and Matisse, maybe stirred not shaken. It is both harsh and sweet. It deals with both love and fear simultanously. She moves fast. I like that the interaction between her and her life models breathes. She does not paint the weight of the waiting. She draws and talks with the paint. She does not treat the painting as an endless hard labour. She treats it as an opportunity to feel free. As she said 'a way to overcome the alienation'. I feel similar. I admire the work's unfinished look, the underkill. When it's over, it's done.

Alice did not die young. Yes, not everything she painted was a masterpiece. But art is not (only) about masters and pieces. It is also about attitude and courage. The unflattering criticism she received about her nude self-portrait at aged eighty, is unforgivably stupid. She painted the most touching paintings of pregnant women that I have ever seen. And, although not consciously, I think my painting *The Painter* (1994) is indebted to and paid hommage to her portrait of Andy Warhol (1970), one of the most beautiful paintings of our century.

1 *Art Since 1900: Modernism, Antimodernism, Postmodernism* (Vol. 2), by Hal Foster, Rosalind Krauss, Yve-Alain Bois, Benjamin H. D. Buchloh, 2005.

Ed van der Elsken

Photographs that like Books and Films that like Photographs

Choosing ten photographs...
I very nearly confined my choice to the only book by Ed van der Elsken that I have in my possession, bought secondhand on the Nieuwmarkt during the late 1970s. That's where I was living at the time, as a twenty-three-year-old art student; Ed used to live there too. It was my first room in Amsterdam, my first book of photographs in the Netherlands, *Bagara*, from 1958. It wasn't so much the individual photographs that caught my eye (aside from that one of the dead little elephant) as their interrelationships and the succession of images, the highly varied sizes and uncommon layout. A lot of deep-black printing ink, no white edges. His photographs of the Banda tribe, famous for their wall paintings, fascinated me. I selected one photograph from this group, a black 'Snow White', sleeping on her bamboo bed, with drawings on the wall behind her.

Hanging on the wall of my studio on the Prinsengracht during the late 1980s, were lots of pictures. Among them, an invitation to an exhibition of Ed's, depicting a photograph of a young woman (Paris, 1954) doubled by the mirror against which she nestles, his muse at the time, Vali. This photograph I'd really like to see again, now with that of a beautiful kiss in which the many arms play a lead role. He found it important to write his own texts for these books of photographs. This fusion of documentation and fiction gives rise to the first docudrama, *Een liefdesgeschiedenis in Saint Germain des Prés (Love on the Left Bank)* (1956) and Vali was now called Ann. The British magazine *Picture Post* changed the ending of Ed van der Elsken's text as his reference to a contracted venereal disease was considered indecent. I decided to use the original last page of this photo novel.

From his big travel book *Sweet Life* (1966) – which included photographs of places such as South Africa, India and Japan – I selected images of the United States and Mexico. It's striking how he deliberately came up with an affectionate title for photographs on not-so-light topics.

The way in which Van der Elsken incorporated photographs, texts and depictions in his films is remarkable. Van der Elsken's final film *Bye* (1990) even includes X-ray photographs of his fatal tumors and his very own commentary on them.

Ultimately my selection had largely to do with artistic expression, with cultural rites and places where art manifests itself: the façade of a Harlem bookstore during the 1960s; the Guggenheim Museum, New York, 1961 – literally and figuratively white – (what a wonderful coincidence that Rineke now has a show there); the winner of a Miss Artist Model Competition (which reminds me of my daughter and which was taken in the year I was born, 1953); two grainy nocturnal photographs (no flash allowed) of Chet Baker's performance at Amsterdam's Concertgebouw in 1955, another of a Mexican religious ritual involving a drunk pilgrim, sleeping on the ground.

Last of all I chose photograph no. 213, which Van der Elsken described in *Once Upon a Time 1925–1990*, as his final photograph: 'the picture I never took.' This invisible photograph is my number ten.

Mike Kelly

Marlene Dumas on Mike Kelley

My first encounter with Mike Kelley was at the Sydney Biennale in 1984. Galerie Metro Pictures in New York had told me about his work because he was an extraordinary talent. I was certainly impressed by his space there, filled with drawings from floor to ceiling. The way they were hung made the space look more like a boy's room decorated with perverse cartoons, than a modern gallery. His work gave me a great deal of pleasure and energy.

The group exhibition *Distemper, Dissonant Themes in the Art of the 1990s*, was held in Washington DC in 1996. There, Kelley talked about his liking for cheap whisky – a taste he remained faithful to, though by then he could afford anthing he wanted. I also learned about his love – one I share – for the melancholy paper cut-outs made by the well-known children's writer Hans Christian Andersen. I listened to passionate exchanges between Kelley and Thomas Schütte, with Kelley arguing that public sculpture had no raison d'être in our present time and should not be made any more. He also felt that artists are not critical enough about taking part in group exhibitions, which profess views to which individual artists don't necessarily subscribe.

Kelley explored concepts that culture, American culture in particular, impose upon us. He projected different personalities in his work that led to confusion as to who he actually was and what he stood for. After his mid-career retrospective at the Whitney Museum in 1993 – resulting partly from the success of his 'abject' art with found soft toys – he felt he was being seen as an abused child. In fact, what he was interested in was the wider spectrum of 'institutional abuse'.

We belong to the same generation, a generation with a predilection for the language of psychotherapy. Kelley himself described it as 'the point at which it becomes glaringly obvious that we are unnatural and that normality is an acquired state'. He also proposed that 'the heroic individual is replaced by a kind of multi-individual': the artist as actor and art as satire. To my mind, Kelley had an affinity with the bitterly self-disparaging German Martin Kippenberger, but also something of Maurizio Cattelan's veiled melancholy. He was a critical but child-like, playful artist.

The stereotypical macho male artist has been replaced by the sensitive man with the courage to deal with the subject of adolescence and look at the world from the perspective of others. Mike Kelley was important not only for representing an art that shines the spotlight on authority, religion, kitsch and our notion of family, but also because he embodied the psychological struggle of the 'accepted' artist in the twenty-first century.

Luc Tuymans

Luc

Luc brought us relief from the loud, large, heavy overload of neoexpressionism of the 1980's, dominated by Germans like Kiefer and Baselitz, and Americans like Schnabel. He offered painting a break from all the romantic mythologies around and brought it back to the real world: the traumatized post-colonial world in need of critical introspection.

Here was a young Belgium guy who started his career by taking on historical subject matter that no contemporary painter dared to touch, not only the Second World War but also the holocaust. He deliberately delivered bare, tonal and undramatic minimal paintings: high anxiety concentrated into an intimate and small scale.

I first saw an exhibition of Luc's work in 1991, called *Disenchantment.* I couldn't place these works in any of the 'ism's' that were around at the time. It wasn't about a 'return to figuration', a plea for 'abstraction' or a flirt with 'sensationalism'. It was actually about disenchantment. Not how it looks, because disenchantment isn't a thing, it's about how it feels. It is about universal psychological truths and at the same time it is about the specific and limited meaning of images as images and confronting that understanding.

I don't find his work impersonal or cool at all. These works vibrate with inner tensions. They brood. They are nervous. Just because he plays the doctor doesn't mean he's not the patient too?! What one finds so disconcerting is not that he is so distant or indifferent, but that despite its unpleasant subject matter, the works show a very vulnerable state of mind. His unexpected moments of tenderness move me. His explanations of sources and intentions I find touching (I am also blamed for talking too much).

In the end his works are not really about the past but about the future. To me they speak of the sad realization that tomorrow we will say yet again, that we did not know and did not see what was happening today.

Natasja Kensmil

Natasja in Wonderland

Sometimes when you dream, you know that you are almost awake and dawn is on its way, and yet you get stuck in a nightmare that keeps on repeating itself. Images of different times spinning around your head in a frenzy, forcing you to go through endless labyrinths of the past, sometimes dressed-up as the future. Or is it the other way around? Gothic versions of stories you've once read somewhere, pictures you saw or tales you've been told in the dark.

Sometimes you are too scared to go to sleep because you get scared of dying. Other times for fear that those you love might disappear or be taken away while you're asleep, or that something 'bad' might befall them, if you fall asleep. Or just the fear of going mad. You don't know anymore what is outer or inner space, clouds pass through and across. Watch out, the cathedral is flat. A film set from a horror movie could fall on you. You are walking through a haunted house in a bewitched landscape. Lines turn into lace. You are in the land of Kensmil.

Whose history is this? What time is it? Victorian times…? Histories like ancestors never die. *Alice in Wonderland* was written in 1865. In 1863 slavery was abolished in the Dutch colony Suriname. This year we celebrated 150 years of Keti-Koti (the chains have been broken!) In 1863 Edvard Munch was born. His father viewed art (rightly so, I'd say) as an 'unholy trade'. He painted alienation and silent screams. Natasha paints silence with noisy scenes. Listen to the sounds of the dead dancing, the rattling of the bones, the music they make.

I recently heard someone quote the German director Werner Herzog. He was filming in the South American jungle in 1982 and was asked to comment on the beauty of the nature around him, 'Ze birds are in misery. I don't zink zey zing, zey just screech in pain.'

And then there is this fragment from the story of the Brothers Grimm, *The Juniper Tree*, 'A bird rises up from a mysterious fire that appears in the tree, like a mist and sings, "My mother she killed me. My father he ate me. My sister Marlinchen, she gathered up my bones. Tweet, tweet, what a lovely bird I am!"'

We are inside *The Crying Light*.

Jan Hoet

Passages

Jan Hoet's dynamism was – and is – wonderful! He was all concentrated energy and passion. His face moved. His body moved. He would move the world for art: box, flirt and lie, whatever it took, because he still believed that art was worth it. But also that life was worth it. He believed this even more strongly than the artists with whom he worked.

Many after him tried to make another show like *Chambres d'Amis* but did not succeed, because they were not really concerned with people who were not interested in art. He was. Nor did they really love the places such people came from. He did.
You can't make a good exhibition in another's house if you don't enjoy both art and the other.

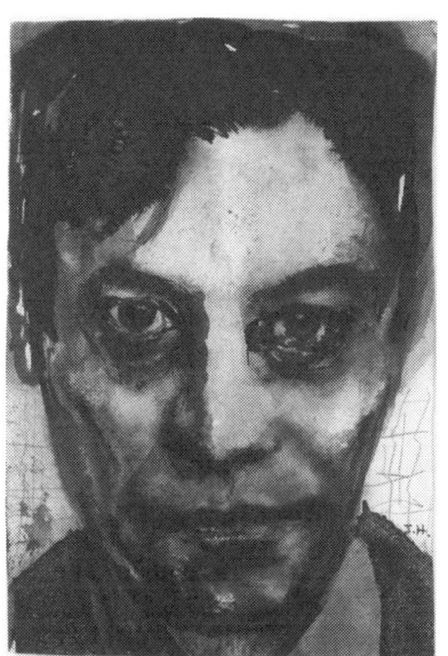

Jan Hoet 1992 20 x 14 cm

Illustrations 1977 – 1993

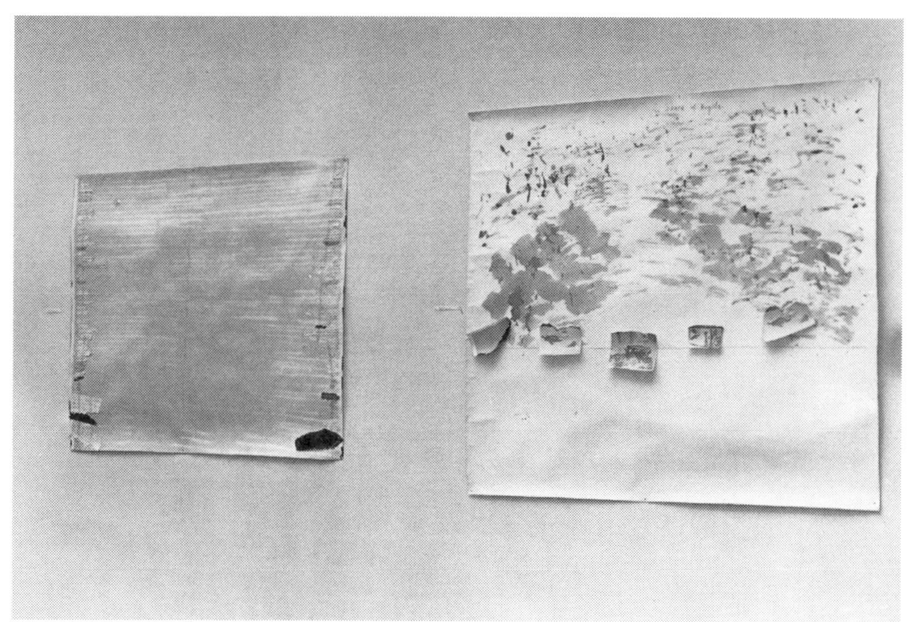

Don't talk to Strangers 1977 125 x 156 cm, *The Death of Angels* 1979 165 x 150 cm

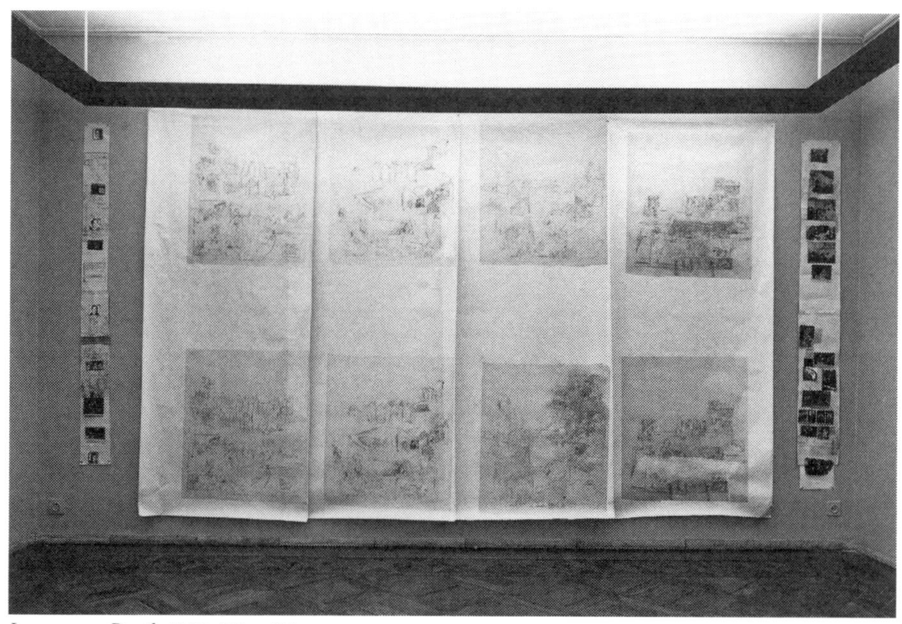

Love versus Death 1980 250 x 400 cm

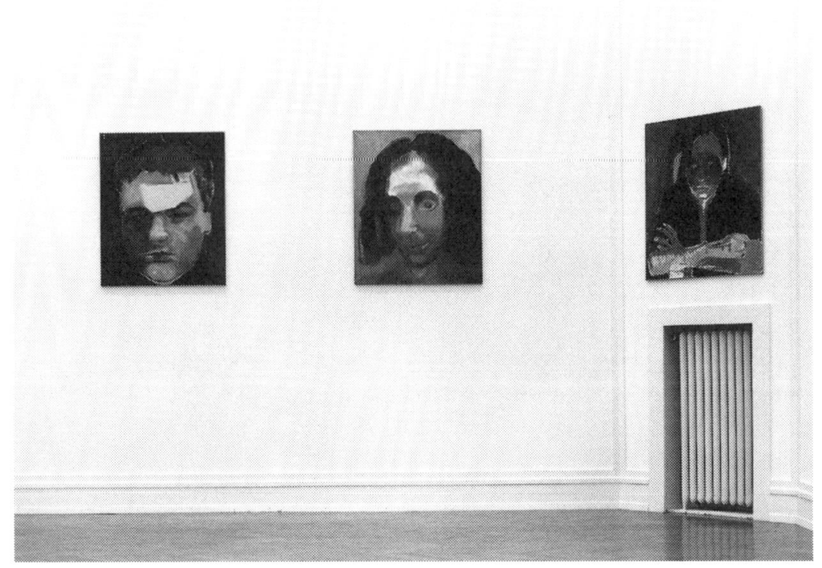

The Accident 1986, *The Jewish Girl* 1986, *Genetiese heimwee* 1984 (3x)130 x 110 cm

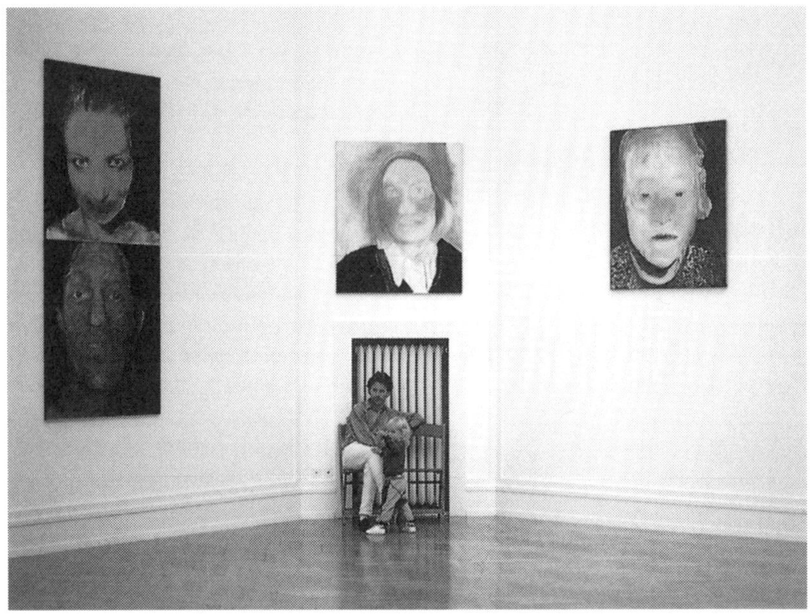

Occult Revival 1984 (2x) 130 x 110 cm, *De vragende vrouw* 1985 130 x 110 cm,
The White Disease 1985 125 x 105 cm

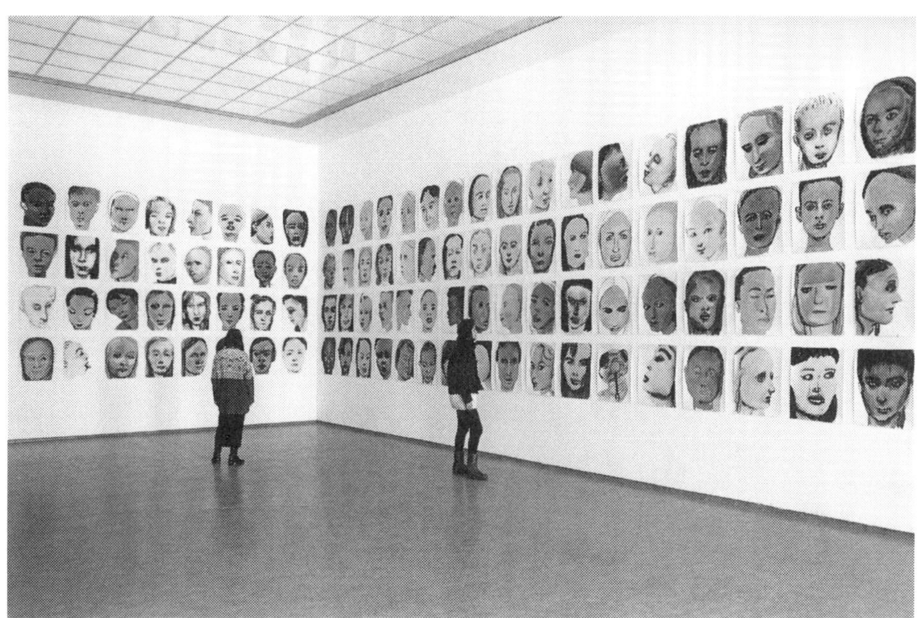

Models 1994 (100x) 62 x 50 cm

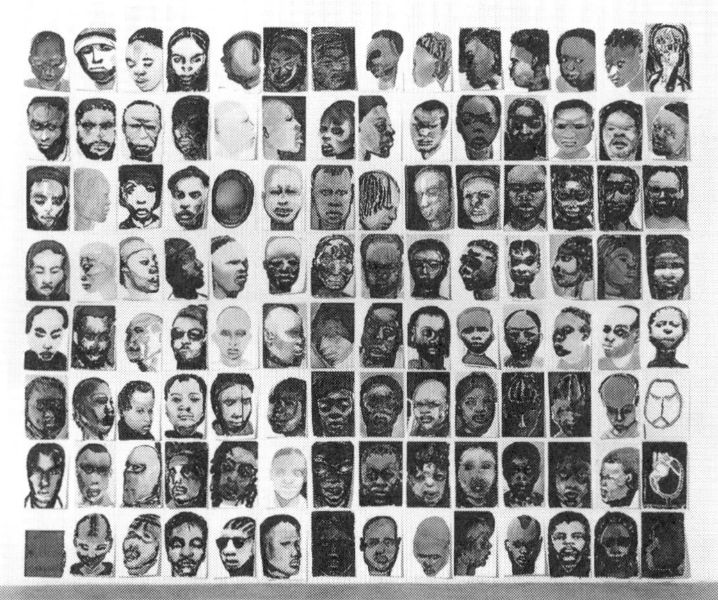

Black Drawings 1991–92 total 221 x 288 cm

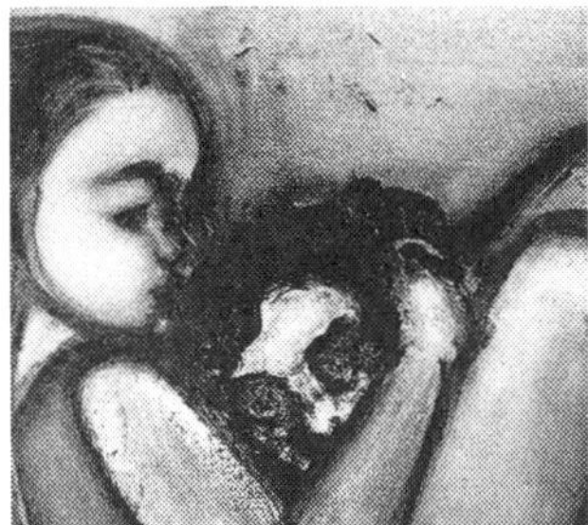

Girl with a Head 1992 25 x 30 cm

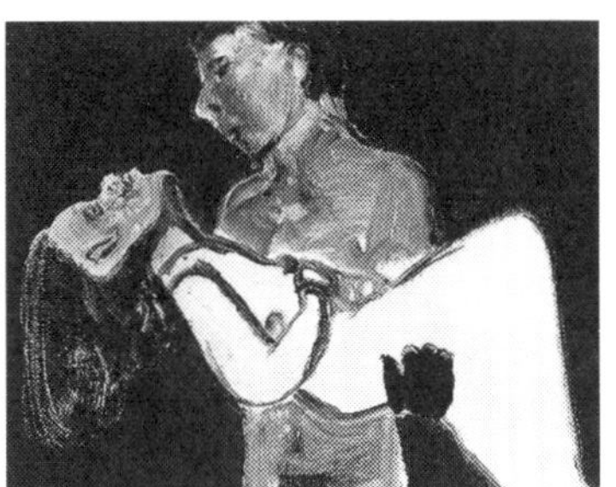

The Image as Burden 1993 40 x 50 cm

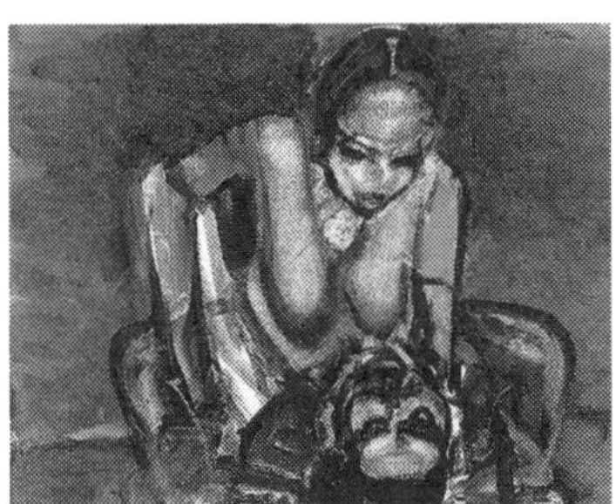

Hierarchy 1992 40 x 55 cm

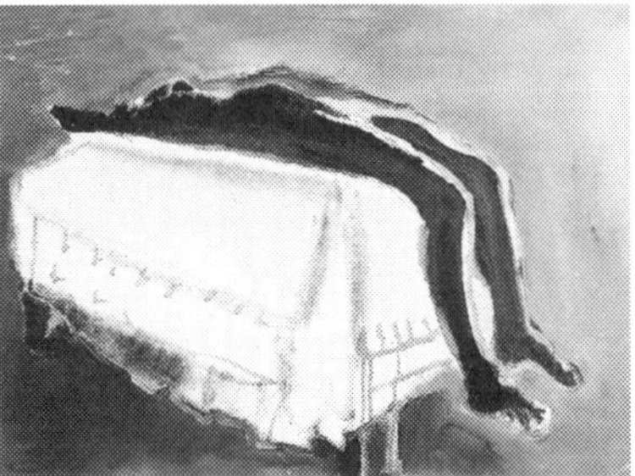

Waiting for Meaning 1988 50 x 70 cm

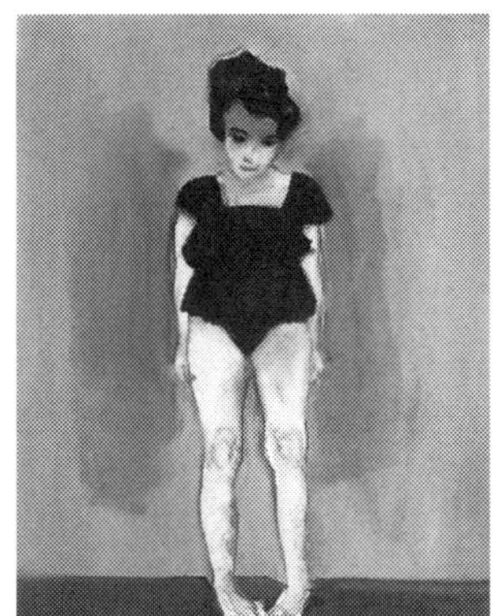

Schaammeisje 1991 60 x 50 cm

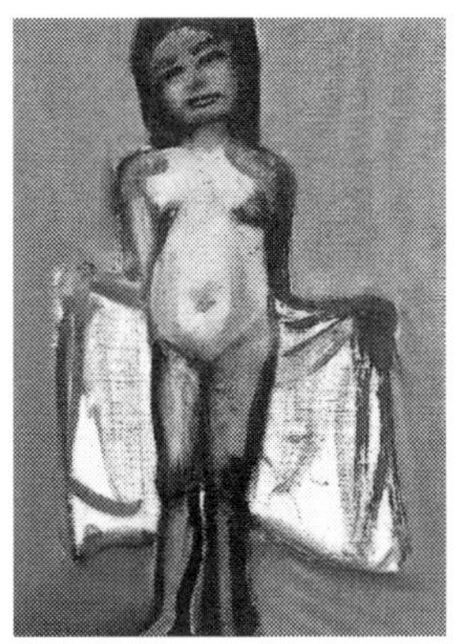

Give the People what they want 1992 40 x 30 cm

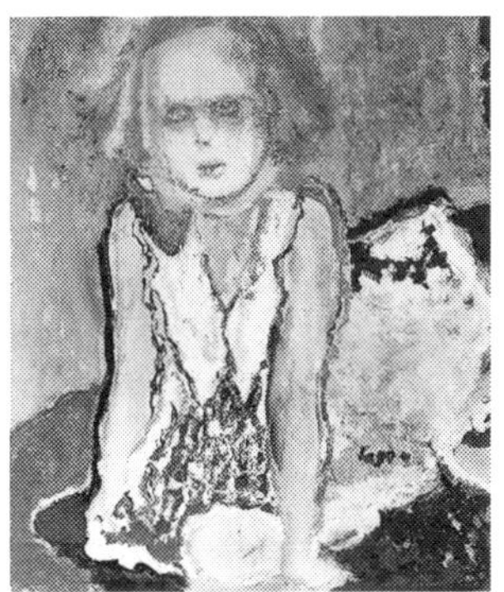

TV Trance 1987 70 x 60 cm

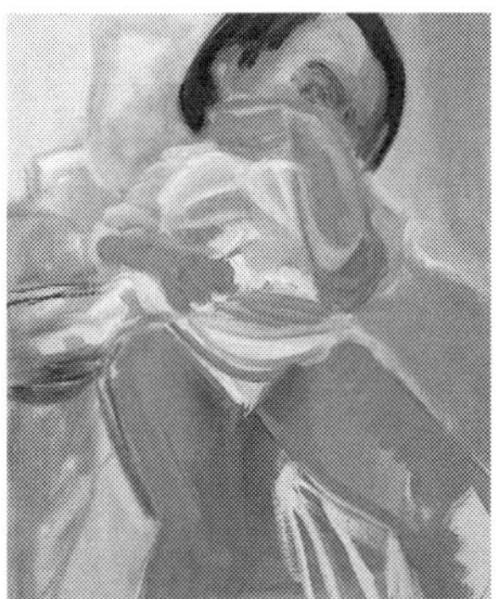

Misinterpreted 1988 60 x 50 cm

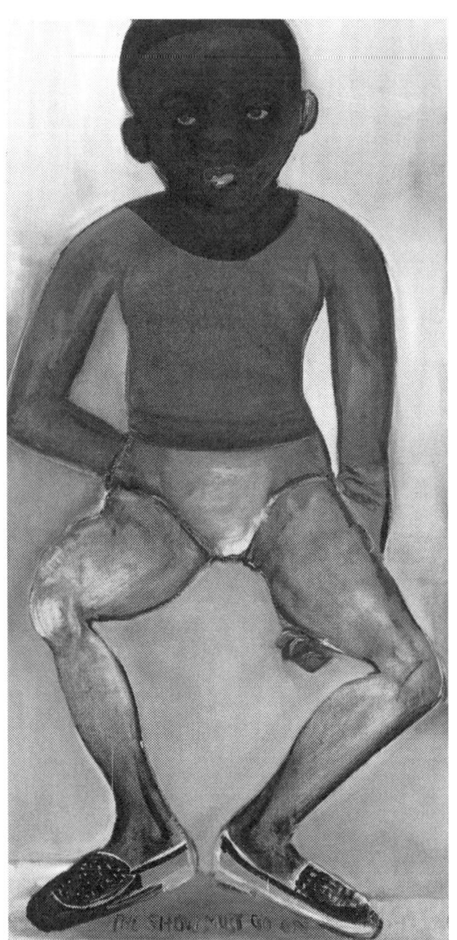

The Show must go on 1991 180 x 90 cm

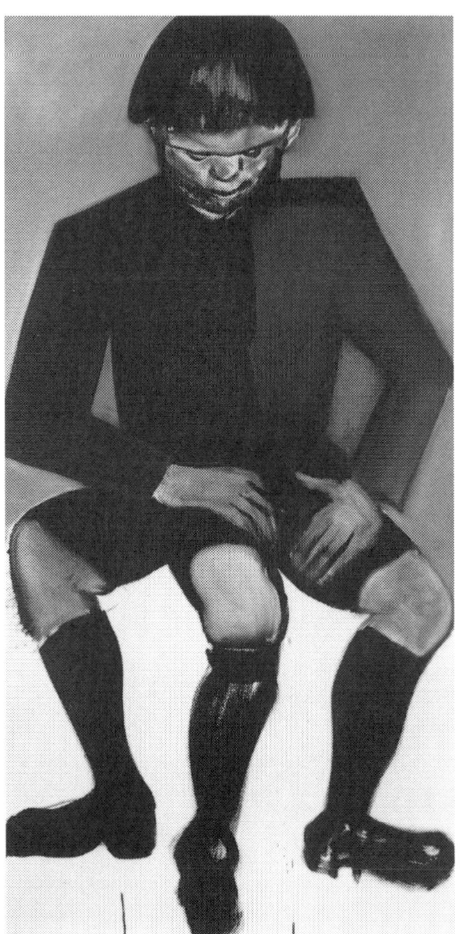

The Human Tripod 1988 180 x 90 cm

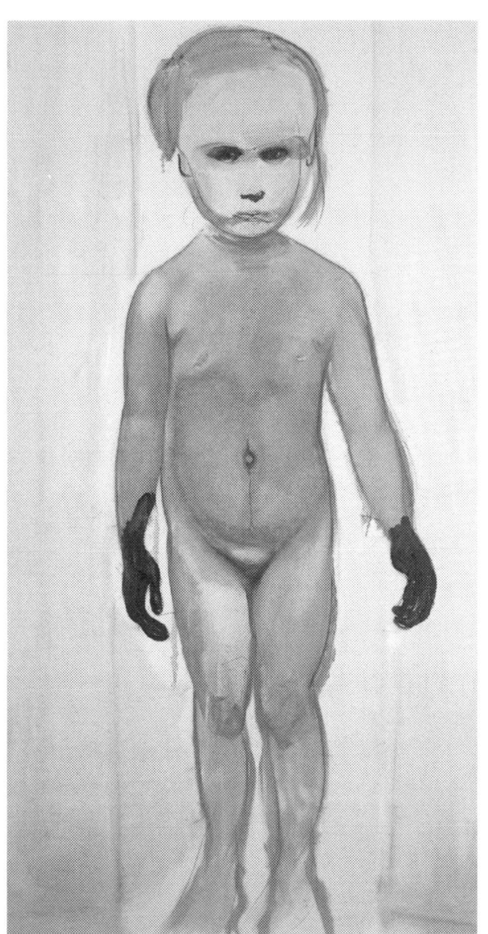

The Painter 1994 200 x 100 cm

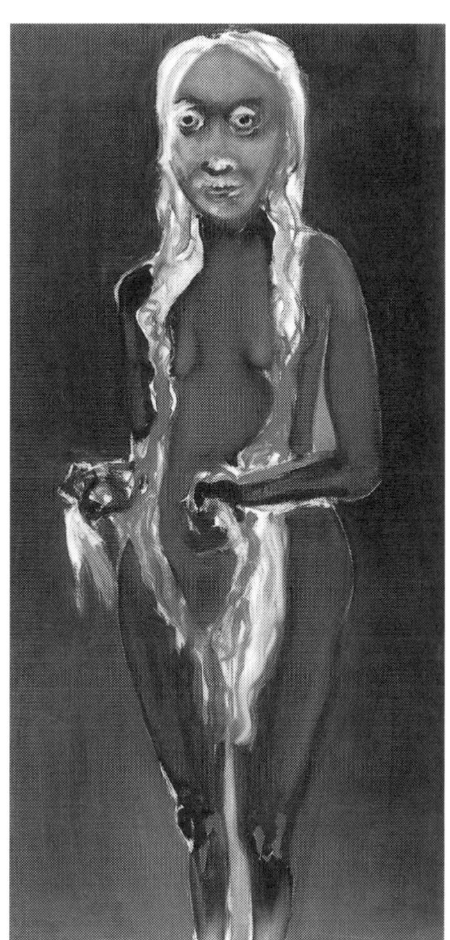

Magdalena 1995 200 x 100 cm

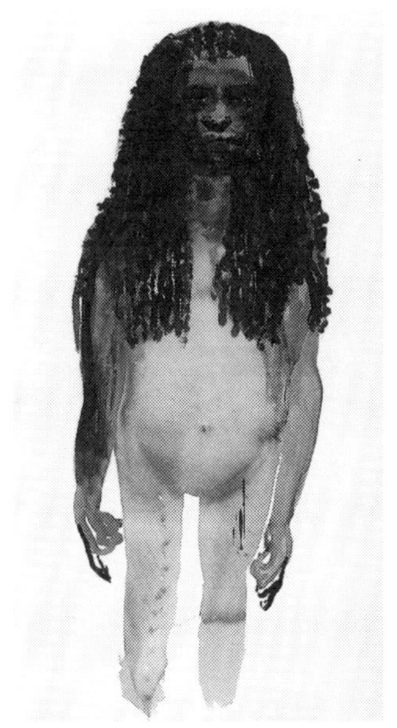

Magdalena (Rasta) 1995 125 x 70 cm

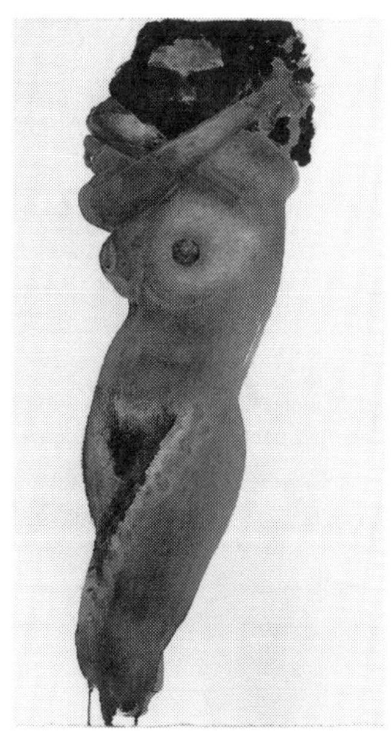

Pin-Up 1996 125 x 70 cm

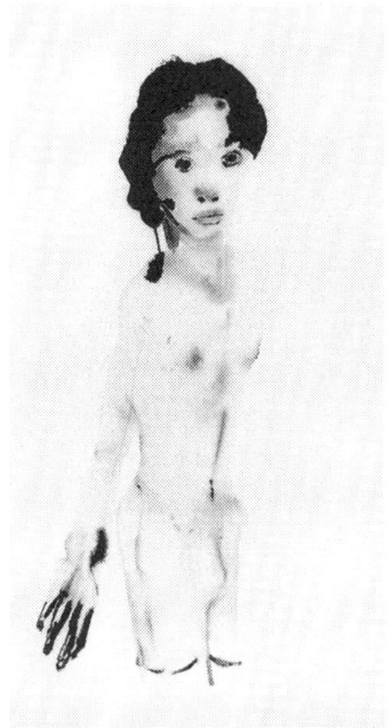

Young Boy (Pale Skin) 1996
125 x 70 cm

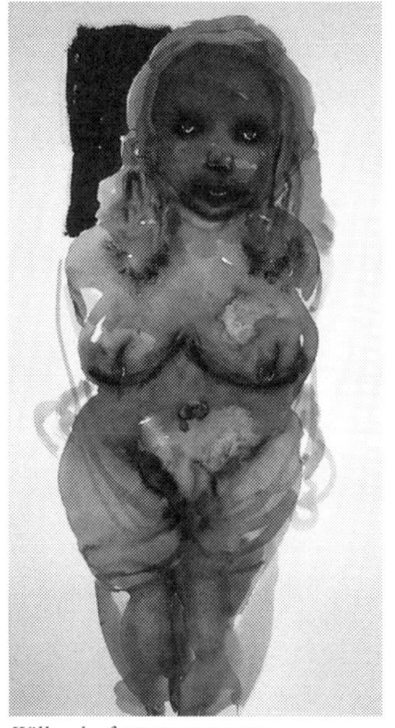

Willendorf 1997 125 x 70 cm

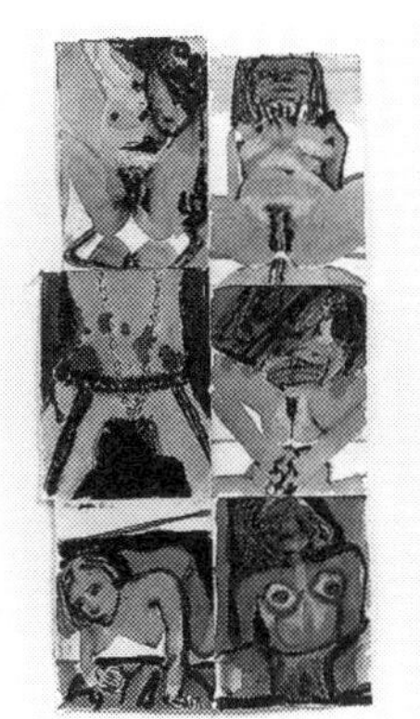

Pornoblues **1993** 200 x 50 cm

Annotations and Sources

Quotation from the *Stedelijk Museum Agenda*, Amsterdam, September 1978.

Why do I write (about Art) was first published in *Kunst & Museumjournaal*, Vol.3, no.4, p.44–46, 1992 (English edition). It was originally written for the symposium *Writing about Art*, held in the Stedelijk Van Abbemuseum, Eindhoven (30.11 – 1.12.1992).

1982

Some Qualities I exhibit, cat. *Junge Kunst aus den Niederlanden, Young Art from the Netherlands, Form und/and Expression*, p.40, Sonderschau Kunstmesse ART 13'82, Basel 1982.

Background was originally published under the title 'Statements' in *Dutch Art + Architecture Today*, no.12, p.14–19, 1982. This is a facsimile in a slightly smaller format.

1983

Love Notes (The Lava-Edge) consists of a selection of texts published in the artist book *The Lava-Edge* (1983), to accompany the exhibition *Reykjavik-Amsterdam ter weerszijden van de meridiaan*, The Living Art Museum, Reykjavik; Museum Fodor, Amsterdam.

1984

Unsatisfied Desire and the untrustworthy Language of Art, cat. *Private Symbol, Social Metaphor*, 5th Sydney Biennale, Sydney 1984.

On Words and Images, cat. *Im Totem Winkel*, p.49, Kunstverein und Kunsthaus Hamburg, Hamburg 1984.

1985

The Eyes of the Night Creatures, cat. *Marlene Dumas, The Eyes of the Night Creatures*, Galerie P. Andriesse, Amsterdam 1985. *A title* and *The aim of my work* are quotations from a text by Paul Andriesse and are taken from a conversation between the author and the artist.

Notes is a translation of *Amsterdamse Notities*, first published in *Fodor*, vol.4, no.4 (July-August), p.38–39, 1985. Originally the text was accompanied by an image of a pin-up playing card and a portrait of Yasser Arafat. The original text is as follows:

Notities

Alleenstaande
Kunst
die slome onkruid
vergroeit mijn tuintje

Waarom vrouwen niet met kunst
kunnen volhouden
Vrouwen zijn gemaakt
in ieder geval
niet om kritiek te vergaren
Dat maakt hun zo
ongelukkig
dat hun het niet
volhouden.

Goede smaak
Behandel mij niet als een kind
jou draak
omdat ik kort en dik ben
en blond geverfd
van aard.
Ik hou jou (verfijnd)
voor de gek.

Name van dinge
Ek benoem die leemtes
door jou
Ek noem dit jou naam
sonder dat jy my vra.

s'Nachts
Vlug
vlieg
die nag weg
verbij
die snelheid van lig.

Onvoorwaardelijk
Onderhandel
niet met mij
het is zoals die man zei:
'Gevangenen kunnen geen
afspraken maken.'

Language Notes, originally published as '2 taalnotities, Amsterdam 1985' (together with '2 liefdesnotities, tijdloos' and '3 katernotities, Amsterdam 1983') in *(ander werk), teksten van kunstenaars in Nederland*, p.33, kaAp, kunst actualiteiten Arnhem produkties, Arnhem 1988. The original text is as follows:

Taalnotitie

Kijk –
mijn woorden
ruik naar ammoniak
en vlek
zonder autoriteit.

Verwerp officiële
gesanctioneerde
TAAL

skrijf
Nederlands
zoals Afrikaans
PRAAT

in slechte aksenten
in onsmaaklijke
onverfijndheden
giegel
zoals meisjies
Hou jou
dom kindjie
en
swaai
jou
Kontje.

The Plague Mentality, cat. *René Daniëls, Marlene Dumas, Henk Visch*, Galerie Barbara Jandrig, Krefeld 1985.

1986

The Intuition of Danger, cat. *Innovation und Tradition / Vernieuwing en traditie*, p.79, Badischer Kunstverein, Karlsruhe 1986.

Fear of Babies was part of an edition of the same title, consisting of 5 lithographs (Ed. 20), produced by Marcel Kalksma, Amsterdam 1986.

Pornograpic Tendency was first published in Dutch #in the cat. *Zeven kunstenaars*, p.10, Galerie Academisch Ziekenhuis Leiden, Leiden 1986. The English version was published in several catalogues and articles. The original Dutch text is as follows:

Mijn kunst
is momenteel gesitueerd tussen de
pornografische neiging om alles
zichtbaar te maken en de erotische
om datgene waarover het eigenlijk
gaat, geheim te houden.

A Girl for all Seasons consists of fragments from the text that was first published as ''n meisje vir alle geleenthede' in *Het Moment*, no.3, p.63–66, Amsterdam 1986.

The original fragments are as follows:

'n Meisjie vir alle geleenthede

Schuld

U zult uit deze uitspraken niets
kunnen controleren en weinig
kunnen voorspellen.
U vraagt misschien:
Wie is er verantwoordelijk voor deze
werken?
U bedoelt waarschijnlijk:
Wiens schuld zijn ze?

Onvrijheid

Ik ben niet gekomen om
de vrijheid te propageren.
Ik ben gekomen om de
ziektesymptomen
van mijn tijd te tonen.
Ik ben een goed voorbeeld van alles
wat fout is met mijn tijd.

Reductie

Reduceer – stil, statisch, sober en
systematisch, zeggen ze,
het universele is niet gediend
met referenties aan het herkenbare,
tijdsgebonden;
noodzakelijkerwijs leidt overdaad tot
ondergang,
het zijn alleen de dommen
die niet van de aarde ontslagen willen
worden,
zeggen ze.

Afstand

Jij – onbekende – behou je afstand.
Ik zoek mijn geluk niet in de
bevrediging,
maar in de intensiteit van de
gevoelens.
En weet dat ik je nooit kan liefhebben
en je altijd vermijd,
om je mijn ogen te besparen.

Titels

Mijn werken (ver)dragen hun namen,
zoals men zijn eigen geschiedenis
moet (ver)dragen.
Dronken van associaties en incest,
besmet met allerlei ziektes en
vooroordelen, opzettelijk verwond,
opdat ze niet hoogmoedig kunnen
worden en hun ingewanden zullen
vergeten.

Geslachtloos

Waar is de erotiek in de kunst van
mijn generatie?
Mijn generatie houdt van
eenzaamheid en
verkiest die zelfs boven seks.
Ze zijn zo sensitief,
ze zijn allergisch voor elkaar.

The Meaning of Drawing consists of a compilation of two texts, respectively: 'The Meaning of Drawing', cat. *The Meaning of Drawing, drawings by ten Dutch artists*, p.46, Netherlands Office for Fine Arts, The Hague 1986; 'The surrealist tradition...' (fragment) taken from the cat. *A Priori tekenen*, p.143, Makkom, Amsterdam 1987.

1987

The Private versus the Public, cat. *Marlene Dumas*, Galerie Paul Andriesse, Amsterdam 1987.
'Notes on the Private versus the Public', 'Notes on my Text' and 'No more Interviews' were handwritten on a leaflet that was handed out separately during the show.

Selling one's Soul to the Devil, cat. *Art from Europe*, p.26, The Tate Gallery, London 1987.

Blind Spots was first published in Dutch as 'Blinde vlekken' in *De Rijksakademie*, Vol.1, no.3 (Nov), p.13, Amsterdam 1987.

1988

Warning is a translation of the text that was first published on the cover of *Introductie Blauwbaard club*, Amsterdam 1988. The original text is the following:

Waarskuwing

Die liefde is nie blind nie
Die verlede gaan nooit dood nie
Alles wat blink is bloed

Naked Bodies, cat. *Waiting (for meaning)*, Kunsthalle zu Kiel & Schleswig-Holsteinischer Kunstverein, Kiel / Schleswig-Holstein 1988.

1989

The Painter kills the Living, cat. *6 Dutch Artists*, Fruit Market Gallery, Edinburgh 1989.

The Return of the Non-dead was first published in a German translation as 'Die Rückkehr der Nicht-Toten', cat. *Prospect 89, Eine internationale Ausstellung aktueller Kunst*, p.59, Frankfurter Kunstverein, Schirn, Kunsthalle Frankfurt, Frankfurt 1989.

Waiting Rooms (need TV), *Beeld, Kunst voor de toekomst*, special issue 'Tekens van Verzet', Vol.4, no.1 (Jan), Amsterdam 1989.

The Question of Human Pink, cat. *Marlene Dumas, The Question of Human Pink*, p. 18, 28, 34, 48, Kunsthalle Bern, Bern 1989. All the texts were printed in Dumas's own handwriting. In the first section, 'Colour', the third line originally was: 'and what about your back-ground?'. 'Paintings of the human Figure' is a facsimile in a slightly smaller format.
German translations of the texts are included at the back of the catalogue.

1990

The Origin of the Species, cat. *Marlene Dumas, The Origin of the Species*, Staatsgalerie Moderner Kunst, Bayerische Staatsgemäldesammlungen München, Munich 1990. The catalogue contains a printing error in the third part of the text. For: 'The relationships between the artworks show missing links which are not severe between...' Read: '... which are most severe'.

Couples, cat. *Marlene Dumas, Couples*, Museum Overholland, Amsterdam 1990.

The World is flat, *Over schilderen/On Painting*, De Balie/De Rijksakademie, p.12–13, Amsterdam 1991.

Terminologies and **Death as Model** consist of fragments from 'De muze is uitgeput', a lecture by Marlene Dumas given on 16 October 1990 in W139, Amsterdam. The complete text was published in *De uitputting van de muze*, p.16–25, Geurt Imanse (Ed.), W139, Amsterdam 1990. The nature of the text has necessitated the selection of fragments. Some sec-tions were subsequently published in an amended form and are also included under separate headings.

The Artwork as Misunderstanding was originally published in Dutch as 'Het kunstwerk als misverstand', cat. *Individu: Duiding, Verboden verbindingen + twijfel-achtige verbanden*, ICC, Antwerp 1991. The English version was frequently reprinted. The original Dutch text is as follows:

Het kunstwerk als misverstand

Er heerst een krisis met betrekking tot Representatie.
Er wordt gezocht naar betekenis alsof het een Ding is.
Alsof het kunstwerk een meisjie is die haar broekie zou moeten uittrekken, zou willen uittrekken zodra de juiste interpretator langs zou komen.
Alsof er een broekie waren die wij zou kunnen uittrekken.

1992

Miss Interpreted, cat. *Miss Interpreted, Marlene Dumas*, p. 26–80, (English edition), Van Abbemuseum, Eindhoven 1992. Most of the texts in the catalogue are included, except those that have been previously published, quotations by others and existing fairy-tales. These are only included where Marlene Dumas makes direct reference to them in her writing. Notes refering to the included sections are printed on the same pages.

My Brain, cat, *AHHA, Brain Internal Affairs*, Beatrixziekenhuis Gorichem, The Netherlands, 1992.

1993

Give the People what they want is a translation of a Dutch text that was published on the occassion of a show at the Zeno X Gallery, Antwerp, in *De Witte Raaf*, p.10, April, Gent 1993.

Female, cat. *Das 21. Jahrhundert, mit Paracelcus in die Zukunft*, p.124, Kunsthalle Basel, Basel 1993.

Drawings and the People who look at them, *Fön*, p.2, no.3 (July/August), Kunsthalle St.Gallen 1993.

The Blonde, the Brunette and the Black Woman was first published (almost integral) in a German translation in cat. *Der zerbrochenen Spiegel, Positionen zur Malerei*, p.154–155, Kunsthalle Wien, Vienna 1993.

Dead Artists consists of fragments from the *Journal zur Ausstellung, Der zerbrochenen Spiegel, Positionen zur Malerei*, p.10, Kunsthalle Wien, Vienna 1993.

Women and Painting, *Parkett*, No.37, p.140, Zürich 1993.

It's as easy as 1, 2, 3 and **How blue can a white Man get?** are the first and last section of a page in *Parkett*, No.38, p.123, Zürich 1993. The other fragments were published on earlier occasions. A German translation of all the fragments is included in *Parkett*.

The Muse is exhausted is an amended version of a fragment from the lecture by Marlene Dumas in the series 'De muze is uitgeput', given on 16 October 1990 in W139 in Amsterdam. It was published in *Parkett*, No.38, p.1, Zürich 1993.

Blind Dates and drawn Curtains, cat. *Marlene Dumas*, Goldie Paley Gallery/Moore College of Art and Design, Philadelphia 1993. The exhibition traveled to The Arts Club of Chicago in Chicago and to the Art Gallery of York University in Toronto. The Arts Club of Chicago published a separate leaflet in which the same text is published.

To Life, cat. *Überleben*, p.72, Bonner Kunstverein, Bonn 1993–1994.

1994

Home is where the Heart is was first published in a French translation in the cat. *Du Concept à l'image, Art Pays-Bas XXe Siècle*, Musée d'Art Moderne de la Ville de Paris, Paris 1994.

Dutch Art was written for a panel discussion on Dutch art held during the exhibition 'Du Concept à l'image, Art Pays-Bas XXe Siècle', Musée d'Art Moderne de la Ville de Paris, 1994.

Not from Here (I), unpublished. It was prompted by the show 'Not from here' at the Jack Tilton Gallery in New York, 1994.

Not from Here (II) was first published in a Spanish translation in *Guia Mensual de las Artes*, no.13, July, Madrid 1994. The following section was also included:

The Cover up

You can't judge a book
by it's cover.
You can't judge
a woman by her lover' ...but
paintings have to be judged
by their covers and lovers.

It was first published as part of the text 'The Blonde, the Brunette and the black Woman', 1993, and is included there.

The Hatred of Others was first published in the cat. *Dialogue with the Other*, p.62, Kunsthallen Brandts Klaedefabrik, Odense, Denmark, 1994. The exhibition travelled to Norrköpings Konstmuseum, Denmark, 1994.

Jesus, the perfect Lover, was first published in the cat. *4 x 1 im Albertinum, Marlene Dumas, Günter Fruhtrunk, Louise Lawler, Marcel Odenbach*, Staatliche Kunstsammlungen, Dresden, 1994–1995. In the cata-logue the text was combined with the following letter to the director of the museum Mr. Ulrich Bischoff:

Dear Ulrich,
I am not so busy with words at the moment. So I give you this sentence from the Bible that is one of the ones I always come back to. My group of drawings that was in New York and that is now in Geneva is called *Betrayal*. And the BODIES of Christ, that will be in Madrid are called *The perfect Lover*. You have the FACES of Jesus... Hope all is well.

Marlene

(The eyes of the man of sorrows and passion.)

Lovesick was first published in the cat. *Chlorosis – Marlene Dumas*, p.8, The Douglas Hyde Gallery, Dublin 1994.

The beginning of Love Stories and the End of cultural Privacy, unpublished, was written for the catalogue of the show *Cocido y Crudo* by Dan Cameron, Museo Nacional Centro de Arte Reina Sofia, Madrid, 19941995.

1995

The next Generation, *Dutch Biennale Bulletin, Africus, Johannesburg Biennale*, Johannesburg 1995.

Beyond the Protection of the Law was first published in a Dutch version in the cat. *Africus, Johannesburg Biennale*, p.186, Johannesburg 1995. The original South African text is as follows:

Buiten Beskerming van die Wet

Kuns wil nie met jou slaap nie
Kuns is nie so goed nie
en
Kuns is nie so lekker nie.
Kuns laat jou koud kry
en
Kuns verklaar jou voëlvry

Three Marias are better than One, selected fragments from cat. *Dumas, Roosen, Van Warmerdam, XLVI Venice Biennale*, Dutch Pavilion (11.6 – 15.10.1995).

Models consists of selected fragments from the cat. *Marlene Dumas, Models*, a coproduction of Salzburger Kunstverein, Salzburg 1995; Portikus, Frankfurt am Main 1995–1996; Neue Gesellschaft für bildende Kunst, Berlin 1996.

1996

The wrong Questions was Marlene Dumas' comment on the following proposal:

'The present climate of art, so plagued by recession, by indecisiveness, by fin-de-siècle desperation, is longing for the counterweight of a powerful stand. In order to urge such a stand, a cross section of internationally known artists is asked to participate in the project *The Intellectual Conscience of Art*. The constitutive question of the project is: What is (at stake in) art in the 90's? By means of this question we would like to invite you, as a representative of the practice of art, to arrive at a confession of ideas. We would like to hear from you if, for example, the intellectual conscience of art is still situated in the responsibility of the form, as in the days of the avant-garde. Or do you think, in these days of Solingen (European Symbol of neo-racism) and the former Yugoslavia, that the conscience of art should serve to point out evil? But perhaps, inspired by the intellectual conscience, you'd rather think of matters such as the restoration of the subject or the aesthetization of everyday life.'

This proposal was formulated by Annette W. Balkema and Henk Slager, editors of the magazine *Lier & Boog*. They put the proposal to 150 artists and their reactions were published in: *Lier & Boog, Series of Philosophy of Art and Art Theory*, vol. II, 1994, 'The Intellectual Conscience of Art', Annette W. Balkema and Henk Slager (eds.).

The following fragment in the editors' 'Transformative Introduction' prompted Marlene Dumas to react after the publication of the special issue.

'(...) After stating the matters at hand, the question of whether a similar dichtomy* could be observed in the artists' positions and attitudes comes to the fore. Of course, from this side there were repudiative reactions as well to the project's constitutive question. These reactions (for example from Marlene Dumas, Arno van de Mark, Rob Scholte) could by and large be explained from the spreading believe in the autonomy of art and/or a regulatory use of the concept of beauty.

* The introduction had previously made mention of two trends evident in the contributions by theoreticians: '(...) Two constructive tendencies can be observed in the contributions of the theorists: 1) In reflecting its foundation, art should particulary adopt a theoretical attitude with respect to the rising new media; 2) Art still has an anthropological task which is often connected with a critical attitude.'

The letter that Marlene Dumas wrote in reaction, stated:

Dear Annette W. Balkema and Henk Slager,

I think it's a pity that you gave an incorrect account of myself and Rob Scholte (I can't speak for Arno v.d. Mark). What the work, as well as our texts, express is the concept of a myriad of meanings, or even – if viewed negatively – a superfluity of meaning. There is indeed no question of the 'autonomy' of the Artwork, but rather of the chameleon-like nature of this cultural object which changes colour as the context changes. Both Dumas and Scholte focus attention on the Rorschach-like nature of Art. Why did I find it so impossible to answer your questions? Because there was no real dialogue. You presupposed certain prejudices that I don't share with you. I don't think art is going through a crisis at all. On the contrary, it's vibrantly alive and driven by a multi-tude of inputs. It goes against my prin-ciples to prescribe what sort of art others should be making. An under-standing of and insight into cultural diversity, coupled with an openness to other points of view, is precisely one of the vital artistic achievements of our time.

I mistrust many artists who make fine-sounding, across-the-board, aesthetic statements which their own, (aesthetic) visual work radically contradicts. Many standpoints pale immediately because of the ineffective political nature of the work. Jean Luc Goddard is on record as saying some-thing like this: 'Culture is bound up with rules. Art is all about the excep-tion to the rule.' That is why I don't want to apply any general rules to art. I don't want to predict or put forward any particular form of art for the new century, because art springs from the specific and not from the general. When I said that I'd rather 'fly' than 'take a stand', I'm alluding to the meaning of the word 'stand', as expressing standing still. I'm not literally intimating that I absolutely never take up a stand (it was intended to be rather more poetic), but flying opens up a different field of vision from standing still. You're dealing with rapidly altering perspec-tives. The artist as a person remains unfortunately rather limited, but an artwork is not a person. (It's a type of pathetic fallacy to confuse the two, in actual fact.)

The perennial dualistic thinking (this or that, instead of this and that) doesn't appeal to me at all. Rather than everything being seen in terms of its opposite pole, it's more a matter of its encompassing, of what was once supposed to be antithetical. It's not simply a matter of a conflict between 'Modernism' and 'Postmodernism', as though nothing else existed. Everyone said they were against Apartheid (in South Africa) in the 1950s, but often failed to understand how the thinking of that time still influences and dominates their own attitudes, in a more abstract meaning of the word. Anyone who has grown up in a back-ground of violence is mistrustful of fine and neatly formulated speeches, or as the man in the Stanley Kubrick film says: 'You talk the talk but do you walk the walk?'!

And then there's also the fact that people are often opposed not so much to what has been said as to the tone in which it is expressed. Often it's not the question itself which is meaningful, but rather who and what 'prompted' the

question. These shifts of emphasis also engender a positive development of our consciousness (something which has always interested me in terms of art and everyday life). At this particular moment, some forms of Art seem more important to me than others, but that's not really the point. I believe that a 'good' artwork has an intrinsic intellec-tual openness. In the words of Umberto Eco: 'I refrain from imposing a choice between them, not because I do not want to choose but because the task of a creative text is to display the contra-dictory plurality of its conclusions, setting the readers free to choose, or to decide that there is no possible choice.' I ask myself why it's presumed that we are now more desperate than before? The individual and the desperation of groups cannot be measured against the artificial end of a century.
Art can't exist without philosophy. A good artwork is a philosophical flight. But between the word and the deed falls the shadow. They cannot function without each other; but where visual art is concerned, the one cannot replace the other.

Marlene Dumas

Goya's The Fates, was originally entitled 'Marlene Dumas on Goya's The Fates' and published in *The Guardian*, Tuesday June 4, 1996, p.10, as a contribution to the series 'A brush with Genius'. Dumas was the 46th artist to be asked to write about a masterpiece and chose 'Las Parcas' by Goya.

The perfect Lover, The absent Lover and the Daughter was written in reaction to questions posed by Catherine Kinley, Assistant Keeper Modern Collection at the Tate Gallery London, on the occasion of Dumas's show in the Tate Gallery which had the same title. The text was amended and published in the cat. *Marlene Dumas*, Tate Gallery London, London 1996.
'Helena said' is an addition and was first published in cat. *Dumas, Roosen, Van Warmerdam, XLVI Biennale di Venezia, Padiglione Olandese*, p.36, Witte de With, Rotterdam 1995.

Pin-Up, consists of selected fragments from the texts in the cat. *Marlene Dumas, Pin-Up*, Stedelijk Museum Het Toreke, Tienen, Belgium, 1996.

Youth and other Demons, cat. *Marlene Dumas, Youth and other Demons, Gallery Koyanagi*, Tokyo 1996.

Masterpieces and Miss World, originally published in Dutch as 'Meesterwerken en Miss Wereld' in *Kunstschrift*, No.6 (Nov-Dec), p.28–29, Weesp, Holland, 1996. The text was followed by a Dutch translation of 'Marlene Dumas on Goya's The Fates' (see **Goya's The Fates**).

1997

First Flights Overseas are selected fragments from Dumas' contribution to *The Bread and Butter Stone, The Douglas Hyde Gallery on Memory*, Jubilee volume, Douglas Hyde Gallery, Dublin 1997.

Rejects and Reasons and **Art and Prostitution** were published in cat. *Auf dem Strich, Arbeiten zum Thema Prostitution*, Kulturviertel im Sophienhof Kiel, Kiel 1997. Originally there was an additional line to the third section of 'Rejects and Reasons': 'These drawings are left-overs from other groups.'

A nice Girl like you, Brigitte Kölle (Ed), *Portikus, 1987–1997*, p. 257, Frankfurt am Main 1997.

The Drive-Inn is a fragment from a text that was written for the film 'Miss Interpreted (Marlene Dumas)' by R. Evenhuis & J. Verhey, MM Produkties, Amsterdam 1997.

Women (unpublished), Amsterdam 1997.
As the World turns is a fragment from Dumas' contribution to: *The Bread and Butter Stone, The Douglas Hyde Gallery on Memory*, Jubilee volume, Douglas Hyde Gallery, Dublin 1997.

Valentines Day and **Always true** were specially written as Epilogue for the first edition of *Sweet Nothings (*1997).

1998

Accepting Painting for what it is. Excerpt from a conversation with Gavin Jantjes. Marlene Dumas replies to Jantjes saying the following: 'There is something the viewer has got to do when he or she looks at your work. You have to look and think beyond first references'. Originally published in *A fruitful Incoherence*, p.50, Iniva, London, 1998,

Improper Relationships. Originally published in *Marlene Dumas*, p.142, Phaidon, London, 1999.

1999

A true Hedonist is hard to find and **MD-light** were originally published in *Marlene Dumas*, M.D., MUKHA | Antwerpen; Camden Arts Center | London; Henie Onstad Kunstsenter | Høvikodden, (cat.), 2000. The exhibition consisted of a group of works previously shown at Frith Street Gallery, London.

Fame and Fortune. Originally published in *Marlene Dumas*, p.138, Phaidon, London,1999.

2000

Never say Never or One Drawing too Many. Selected fragments from *Marlene Dumas: One hundred Models and Endless ReJects*, (cat.), Institute of Contemporary Art, Boston, 2001.

2001

Name no Names and **Topless Bars and Structural Skeletons** are selected fragments from *Marlene Dumas, Nom de Personne/Name no Names*, (cat.), p.34–37, Cabinet D'Art Graphique, Centre Pompidou, Paris 2001.

2002

Wake-up Call and **You know you are a Foreigner** are extracts from *Early Works, De Ateliers* 1998 – 2002, (cat.) p.20–21, Amsterdam 2002.

2003

Suspect, Simplicity and **About Heaven** are selected fragments from *Marlene Dumas Suspect* (cat.), p.35, 46, 66, 77, 79, Palazzetto Tito, Venice 2003. The three rooms that are mentioned in the text refer to the different rooms in the exhibition. *About Heaven* and *Simplicity* are written on works on paper with the same name. *About Heaven* dates from 2001. Here – and in the catalogue *Suspect* – it is presented in combination with related fragments dating from 2003.

2004

The Right to be Silent, The Death of the Author and **Immaculate** were written for and originally published in *Frieze*, issue 80 – A special edition for the Frieze Art Fair, p.84–89, 2004.

The Second Coming. Selected fragment originally published in Marlene Dumas: The Second Coming, (cat.), Frith Street Gallery, London, 2004.

2005

Pretty Boys Originally published in *Respect! Forms of Community: Contemporary art From the Netherlands*, (cat.), Marrakech, 2005. There it was preceded by a quote from a Dutch rap song by Ali B:

Even lekker stappen had voor hem geen zin
Dat was de reden waarom hij ook altijd buiten hing
Lekker chillen met zijn matties hij deed zijn ding
Ging niet naar een discotheek want hij kwam er niet in
(uit: *Geweigerd*, Ali B)

2006

Man Kind. Written for the exhibition *Man Kind*, Galerie Paul Andriesse, 2006, and originally published in *Contra o Muro. Marlene Dumas* 2010 (cat.). p.73, Museu Serralves, Porto, 2010.

And God said – I told you so. Written for and originally published in *Kitsch Unedited. Letters and texts of friends* compiled by Jan Andriesse, De Pont Museum of Contemporary Art, Tilburg, 2006.

2007

On Photography and modern Life. Selected fragments from a conversation between Marlene Dumas and Ralf Rugoff. Originally published in *The Painting of Modern Life*, Hayward Gallery, London, 2007.

Adult Entertainment or what do I do (when you are far away). Artist's statement dating from 1986, originally published in *Intimate Relations*, (cat.) Jacana Media | Johannesburg & Roma Publications | Amsterdam, 2007.

2008

Hommage to the Polaroid, Measuring your own Grave, Framing and Naming, Southern Comfort, North Africa (Woman of Algiers), Beaches ain't what they used to be and **Expiring Dates** were all written for and originally published in *Marlene Dumas, Measuring your own Grave*, (cat.), The Museum of Contemporary Art, Los Angeles, p.91, 194, 261, 179, 177, 179, Los Angeles, 2008. **Expiring Dates** was originally published with the title *Expiration Dates* in a version without the line '11 September 1990 – George Bush Sr. declared war against Iraq'. The text was also included in *Marlene Dumas*, p.206, Phaidon, 1999, there without the line '11 September 2001 – Hijacked jetliners hit the World Trade Centre in New York, destroying the Twin Towers'.

2009

The Third World War. Translated version of ' De Derde Wereldoorlog' originally published in Dutch in Metropolis M, 2009–2010, issue 6, page 17; online: metropolism.com/magazine/2009-no6/de-derde-wereldoorlog/

2010

Contra o Muro. Originally published in *Contra o Muro. Marlene Dumas* 2010 (cat.), p.57, Museu Serralves, Porto, 2010.

Against the Wall. Letter to David. Extract, original text published in *Against the Wall*, (cat.) p.49–55, David Zwirner with Radio Books, New York, 2010.

Two of a kind. Originally published in Contra o Muro. Marlene Dumas 2010 (cat.), p.59, Museu Serralves, Porto, 2010.

For Whom the Bell tolls. Originally published in *Contra o Muro. Marlene Dumas* 2010 (cat.), p.80, Museu Serralves, Porto, 2010.

2011

A gothic Story. The final Tale. An edited compilation of previously published texts *A Gothic Story* and *A Final Tale*. *A Gothic Story* was originally published in *Marlene Dumas: Negotiating small Truths*, (cat.) Jack S. Blanton Museum of Art, University of Texas, Austin,1999. *A Final Tale* was originally published in *Me and the Queen*, (cat.), Koninklijke Prijs voor de Schilderkunst | Royal Award for Painting, 2011.

Royal Awards: Queens, Stars and Painters. Selected fragment of Me and the Queen, (cat.), Koninklijke Prijs voor de Schilderkunst | Royal Award for Painting, 2011.

2012

Every Prize has its Price. Edited version of the speech given by Marlene Dumas during the award ceremony of the Johannes Vermeer Prize 2012 on 29 October, Museum Het Prinsenhof, Delft, The Netherlands, 2012.

An Artwork of the 19th century that was and stays important to me. Even Fairies can be ok. Originally published in *Frieze Masters. Ideas from the past in the art of the present*, p.87, 2012. Published on the occasion of the Frieze Art Fair 2012.

2014

Non-traditional Relationships. Written for and originally published in Manifesta 10, The European Biennal of Contemporary Art (cat.), St Petersburg, 2014.

Politics (of Art) 1989 –1997

From one dirty Place to Another, *Galerie Innodiging voor mooie tentoonstellingen + Trio eenzaamheid*, p.40, Paul Andriesse, Amsterdam 1989.

The Art of Exhibiting. Sections 1 to 5 formed Marlene Dumas' written reaction to a forum debate organized by the Netherlands Office for Fine Art (Rijksdienst voor Beeldende Kunst) and prompted by the book *L'Exposition imaginaire*. Dumas did not participate in the debate and her comments were not broached. They were finally published in *Metropolis M*, no. 3, p.16–17, Utrecht 1990, with section 6 and the following text (originally in Dutch) as addendum:

A brief elucidation of the already com-pact statements is virtually impossible. So here are a couple of additions. The criticism is also aimed at myself and at artists in general who are rather too passive in their attitude.

Artworks are outlawed objects, delivered up to the amusement and estimation of strangers. Even if I wanted to, I cannot strip the images of this double-edged freedom. But that is exactly the reason why discussion about the banners under which we bring together ideas, or rule others out, is an essential part of the whole exhibition issue. Artists are usually only brought-in on an exhibition after the show's basic premise has already been decided. And because many concepts are vague and broad, everyone can find some-thing they respond to (somewhere) in them. In itself, I used to think that was no bad thing. But now I perceive 'no bad thing' as 'no good thing'. But I'd like to ask exhibition-makers not to remain in the background, but rather to strive to formulate their motivation and attitudes in a more sharply focused way. And that goes for the artists as well. This divergence between artist and exhibition-maker (when they are two different people) might lead to less being taken for granted or even to fewer shows. Nobody is served by an excess of nice exhibitions, their catalogues burgeoning into butter-mountains of superfluity.

My Thoughts on big Shows, cat. *Documenta IX*, p.140, Kassel 1992. In the catalogue the last section was in Dutch:

Geef mij het hoofd van Johannes de Doper.

Bacon and Dumas, or the Discomfort of being 'coupled', cat. *Marlene Dumas – Francis Bacon, The Particularity of being Human*, Malmö Konsthall, p.27–39, Malmö 1995; cat. *Marlene Dumas – Francis Bacon, The Particularity of being Human*, Castello di Rivoli, p.27–39, Turin 1995.

Deadlines and Airmiles, (unpublished) was written for a special issue of *Parachute* (Fall 1995) on the theme of transit.

International Biennales, statement held at the press conference of Manifesta on March 22, 1996 and published in cat. *Manifesta*, p.7–11, Rotterdam 1996. The texts were introduced both in the statement and publication by the following section:

Firstly I want to state that I didn't have any part in selecting the curators, or the Advisory Board or the artists. I do however support the aims of this manifestation and the dreams of the organisers and co-ordinators. I do have to mention Jolie van Leeuwen and Hedwig Fijen, because without them there would not be no foundation on which all the interactions can take place.

The 7 Year Itch, *Art Gallery Exhibiting, The Gallery as a Vehicle for Art*, p.177, Paul Andriesse/De Balie 1996. 'The 7 Year Itch' was published alongside 'From one dirty place to another'(see above).

A united Europe, (unpublished), Amsterdam 1997.

Do the right Thing, was written for the yet unpublished *Grey Areas: Representation, Politics and Identity in Contemporary South African Art*, B. Atkinson & C. Breitz (Eds.). The text will be published in the book in a slightly different form.

On Others 1986 –2014

Two texts addressing the work of other artists were already included in the first edition (1998) **Bacon and Dumas, or the Discomfort of being 'coupled'** (1995) was included under Politics (of Art), for the annotation see p.243. Also **Goya's The Fates** (1996) was included before, for the annotation see p.240. Both remained in their original position.

Erik Andriesse | **Nightmares of Beauty.** Written in 1986 and originally published in *Erik Andriesse (1957–93)*, (cat.) Erik Andriesse Foundation, Amsterdam, 1998.

Lidwien van de Ven | **The Body Guard**. Originally published in *Kapriolen: Zeitgenössische Kunst aus die Niederlanden*, (cat.), Kunstverein, Munich, 1989.

Jan Andriesse | **The Tyranny of Reality and the autonomy of Painting** Originally published in *Jan Andriesse*, (cat.) Galerie Maria Wilkens, Köln, 1989

Jan Andriesse | **Future Perspective, or why he's not the Man they say he is**. Written in 1999 for – and originally published in – *Jan Andriesse*, Dordrechts Museum, (cat.) Dordrecht, 2000. As this text is a sequel to the text above, it is placed in relation to it, instead of chronologically under 1999.

Anton Corbijn | **Live Acts. Silent Studios**. Originally published in *Anton Corbijn | Marlene Dumas | strip-pinggirls*, (cat.), Theatermuseum Amsterdam, SMAK Gent, Institut Neerlandais Paris, 2000.

Frank Stella | **Notes on All is Fair in Love and War.** Previously unpublished. Written on the occasion of the exhibition *All is Fair in Love and War* at Jack Tilton | Anna Kustera Gallery, New York, 2001.

Vincent van Gogh | **As good as it gets. Van Gogh is the One**. Originally published in *Vincent van Gogh and Contemporary Art*, (cat.), Van Gogh Museum, Amsterdam, 2003.

Marijke van Warmerdam | **Tomorrow.** Originally published in *M+M Marlene Dumas, Marijke van Warmerdam*, (cat.) Montevergini, Siracuse, Italy & BAWAG Foundation Wien, Osterreich, 2004.

p.s. Exhibiting in Dangerous Places. In Sicily you have to watch out for the mafia, in Vienna you have to watch out for the Freudians …

Melissa Gordon | **Collateral Damage**. Originally published in *Wild at Heart*, (cat.), De Ateliers, Amsterdam, 2006.

Keren Cytter | **Improvise. Lalala and Halloo**. Originally published as 'On the drawings of Keren Cytter' in *Keren Cytter*, (cat.), MUMOK | Museum Moderner Kunst Stiftung Ludwig Wien, 2007.

Jean Auguste Dominique Ingres | **The Portrait of Joséphine Éléonore Marie Pauline de Galard de Brassac de Béarn, Princesse de Broglie.** Originally published in Dutch in *Nexus*, Nr.55, May 2010.

Alice Neel | **Alice doesn't live here anymore**. Originally published in *Alice Neel. Painted Truths*, (cat.), Museum of Fine Arts Houston, 2010.

Ed van der Elsken | **Photographs that like Books and Films that like Photographs.** Written on the occasion of the exhibition *LOOK ED! Vintage photographs by Ed van der Elsken* selected by Marlene Dumas, Rineke Dijkstra and Marijke van Warmerdam, Annet Gelink Gallery, Amsterdam, 2012 . Translation Beth O'Brien.

Mike Kelley | **Marlene Dumas on Mike Kelley**. Originally published in Dutch in the special edition of NRC Handelsblad, issued 13 December 2012, on the occasion of Mike Kelley's solo exhibition at the Stedelijk Museum in Amsterdam. Translation Yvette Rosenberg.

Luc Tuymans | **Luc**. Written for and partly published in *Luc Tuymans Allo!*, by Skye Sherwin in *AnOther Magazine*, London, October 18, 2012.

Natasja Kensmil | **Natasja in Wonderland**. Originally published in *The Crying Light*, (cat.), Royal Hibernian Academy Dublin, 2013.

Jan Hoet | **Passages**. Originally published – in a slightly altered form – as *Jan Hoet 1936 – 2014* in *Art Forum*, Summer 2014.

Index

D

E

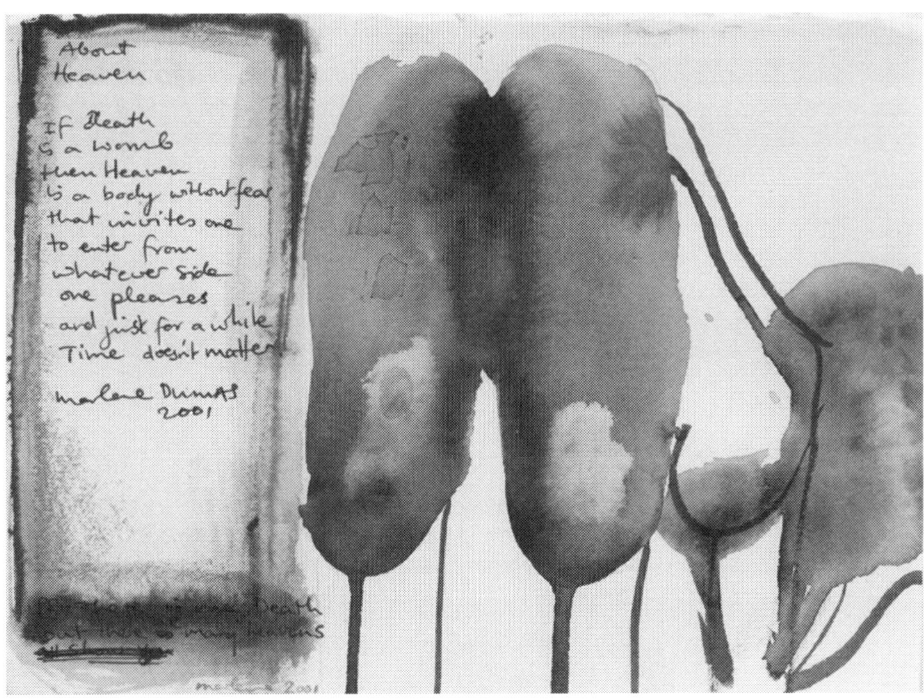

About Heaven 2001 160 x 220 cm

Biography

Marlene Dumas was born in 1953 in Kuilsrivier, South Africa. She attended Michaelis School of Fine Art in Cape Town from 1972 to 1975. In 1976 she came to the Netherlands on a scholarship and spent two years studying at Ateliers '63 in Haarlem. Marlene Dumas has taught at several art institutions in the Netherlands and gave many guest lectures abroad. She lives and works in Amsterdam. Although she has had Dutch nationality since 1989, she once said:

'Someone once remarked that I could not be a South African artist and a Dutch artist, that I could not have it both ways. I don't want it both ways. I want it more ways'.

Her work has featured in leading international exhibitions including Documenta VII and IX (Kassel, 1982 and 1992), *Der Zerbrochene Spiegel, Positionen zur Malerei* (Vienna and Hamburg, 1993) and *Distemper, Dissonant Themes in the Art of the 1990s* (Washington DC, 1996). Other important exhibitions devoted to painting in which Dumas was represented include *Trouble Spot: Painting* (1999), *Painting at the Edge of the World* (2001) and *The Painting of Modern Life* (2007). Her work has also featured in exhibitions with a focus on Africa, such as the *Africus Biennale* in Johannesburg (1995) and in *Africa Remix* (2004–2006).

Dumas's work has also been showcased in solo exhibitions in many museums both in the Netherlands and abroad. Solo exhibitions in the Netherlands include the Centraal Museum Utrecht (1984) and the Van Abbemuseum in Eindhoven (1992). Abroad they include the Kunsthalle Bern (1989) the Institute of Contemporary Arts in Philadelphia (1993), and the Institute of Contemporary Arts (1993) and the Tate Gallery (1996), both in London. In 1995 her work, together with that of Maria Roosen and Marijke van Warmerdam, formed the Dutch contribution to the Venice Biennale. In 2001 the Centre Pompidou in Paris staged the first retrospective of her works on paper under the title *Nom de Personne*. The exhibition subsequently featured in the New Museum, New York and the De Pont Museum in Tilburg, under the title *Name no Names*. Between 2007 and 2009 an overview of her oeuvre, in varying combinations, toured three continents. Sequentially *Broken White* was shown in Japan, *Intimate Relations* in South Africa, and *Measuring Your Own Grave* at the Museum for Contemporary Arts in Los Angeles, the Museum of Modern Art in New York, and The Menil in Houston. In 2010 the Fundacao Serralves in Porto showed an ensemble of her works in the show called *Contra o Muro*. In 2014 the Stedelijk Museum in Amsterdam launched a retrospective of her entire oeuvre with the title *The Image as Burden*. This comprehensive show is co-produced with the Tate Modern in London and Fondation Beyeler in Basel, and will be presented there in 2015 in slightly different compositions.

Marlene Dumas has received several awards and honours. In 1998, specifically for her drawings, she received the David Roell Prize | Prince Bernhard Cultural Prize for Visual Arts. In 2010, she received an Honorary Doctorate from the Faculty of Humanities, Rhodes University, Grahamstown, South Africa. Her entire oeuvre was awarded the Dutch State Prize for the Arts, the Johannes Vermeer Award, in 2012.

www.marlenedumas.nl

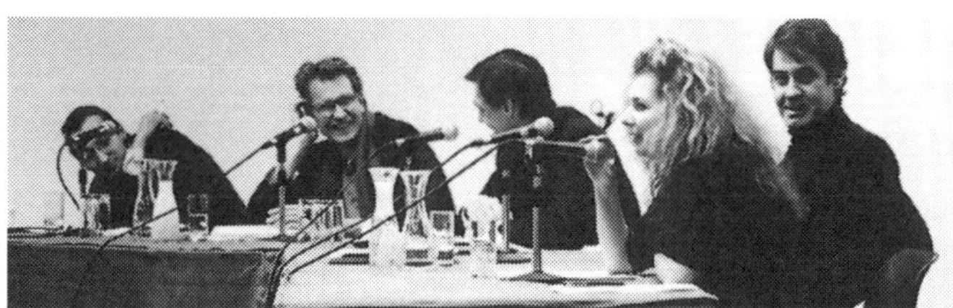

Juan Muños, Niek Kemps, Frank Lubbers, Marlene Dumas, Ludger Gerdes
Symposium *Writing about Art*, Stedelijk Van Abbemuseum, Eindhoven, 1992

Editor's Note

Marlene Dumas' writings have appeared in various catalogues and all sorts of publications over the last decades, nevertheless by now many are difficult to trace. This is unfortunate as Dumas' writing – ranging from aphorisms and short poetic pieces to larger essays – is fascinating material, and provides valuable information on her work from the best possible source. The fact that she also addresses many of the questions which, over the years she has been asked time and again, prompted the gathering of an anthology. *Sweet Nothings* – the result of a close collaboration with the artist – offers a selection of her best and most representative texts and notes, from 1982 to 2014.

Revised and enlarged Edition

Sweet Nothings was first published in 1998. This second (2014) edition, includes the entire first edition – slightly revised in terms of copy-editing and sequence – with the addition of a selection of texts and notes dating from the period between 1998 to 2014.

Selection of the Material

For both editions a thorough inventory of Dumas' texts was drawn up and a wide variety of material was selected, based on the following criteria.

Firstly, material was sifted for inclusion based on whether Marlene Dumas had actually written the text herself. During her entire career, quotations based on hearsay assumed a life of their own, and are repeatedly quoted as Dumas' own words. Only writings by Dumas herself are included in the anthology.

Virtually all the writing was prompted by specific occasions – the exhibition (and catalogue) of a group of works; the publication of an edition; a request for a contribution to a magazine, newspaper or symposium; or an exchange of letters. The degree to which a text could speak for itself and its relevance outside its original framework were important criteria in deciding whether or not to include it.

Also the text's degree of articulateness proved a decisive factor, when faced with a choice between several texts dealing with the same or a similar subject. Mostly the choice was for one or the other, although small overlaps were permitted when for example, we wished to underpin correlations.

Based on the first criterion, interviews in principle do not form part of this anthology, although some telling fragments are included, here authorized by Dumas herself[1]. Also lectures were not included, because they were never written down in advance, but improvised on the spot in relation to the selected visual material. Nevertheless two exceptions were made, both authorized by Dumas[2]. One of them, her speech written for the ceremony of the Johannes Vermeer Award in 2012: a passionate plea for the arts and art education, at a time when the arts in the Netherlands are under attack. It is a meaningful and much quoted text that has an important place in this anthology.

Most texts have been included in their entirety although some writings have been edited, shortened or only fragments of the original included. Details per text are given in Annotations & Sources, where the source, year and place of the first publication can be found, as well as the extent to which the text was edited and any other relevant details.

Organization of the Material

The first edition (1998) of the book was divided into two main sections. The first and largest section contained Marlene Dumas' writings on her own work, and on art and painting in general. Collected together under the heading Politics (of Art), the second section contained contributions relating to (the politics of) galleries, museums and other institutions, duo and group exhibitions, etc. Politics (of Art) covered the peripheral conditions of art. The entire book had been arranged in chronological order with no distinction made as to the form of the contributions. In cases where a text was written earlier than the year in which it was first published, we have kept to the date when it was actually written. An extensive index was, and is again included at the back of the book, making it possible to search by theme or keyword within this chronological structure.

In this second edition (2014), the basic outline of the first edition has been maintained, as a chronological sequence of the texts provides the most natural order, preserving their correlation with the developments within the artist's visual work[3]. All selected writings from 1997 until now, found to be relevant to the first section of her work are placed in direct connection to the previous material[4].

The former section, Politics (of Art) has not been followed up. The reason for this is not that the institutions and machinations of the art world are no longer of interest to Marlene Dumas, but that 'the periphery of art' addressed in the first edition under the heading Politics (of Art), have since 1997 been to a much lesser extent the subject of her writing. It is not the case that her writings have become less 'political', they have always been of a political nature and her references to the current international political situation might even be considered more direct than in previous years; the imaging concerning the conflicts in the Middle East – and its repercussions elsewhere – are the subject of several recent works and texts. These texts, however, are so closely interwoven with the artworks that they belong to the section with texts on her art. Hence this separate category Politics (of Art) has become unnecessary in the second edition.

On Others – a new section in this enlarged edition – has been added, as Marlene Dumas has written extensively on the work of other artists, with most of whom she feels a close affinity. These texts – also chronologically ordered – date from between 1986 and 2014, the last being an obituary for Jan Hoet, the only museum director and curator in this company[5].

Presentation

The present anthology consists of English texts, as the majority of these were originally written and published in English. Of a few texts, originally written in Dutch or South African, an English translation is included, authorized by Dumas herself. In those cases the complete original text has been published as well in the Annotations & Sources. Other texts have been published in a German or French translation as well, reference to these translated versions are made in the Annotations & Sources. An important basic premise underpinning this book was to present the texts in such a way as to allow them to stand on their own. However since Marlene Dumas makes regular references to her artworks in her writing, reproductions of a number of them were assembled in a separate visual supplement at the back of the first edition. In the second edition some reproductions of artworks are printed in relation to the texts. The separate visual supplement however has not been extended, as images of Dumas' works are at present easily accessible, not only in the many catalogues and other publications on her work since then, but also on her website and many others on the internet.

Mariska van den Berg
Amsterdam, September 2014

1 Fragments of the following interviews are included: quotations from an interview with Paul Andriesse have been included with Dumas' permission as *A Title and the aim of my Work* under the heading *The Private versus the Public* (1987). *Accepting Painting for what it is*, is an excerpt from a conversation with Gavin Jantjes, originally published in *A fruitful Incoherence*, London, 1998. And *On Photography and modern Life*, consists of fragments from a conversation with Ralf Rugoff, originally published in *The Painting of Modern Life*, London, 2007.

2 *Terminologies and Death as Model* (1991) are taken from an unpublished lecture by Dumas, which was punctuated by improvisation and anecdotes. These are heavily edited fragments. *Every Prize has its Price* (2012), was written and presented by Marlene Dumas on the occasion of the ceremony of the Johannnes Vermeerprijs. It is the only selected text after 1998 that would have fitted the category Politics (of Art). It has been included in the sequel of the first section on the work.

3 The exception concerns two texts by Jan Andriesse. T*he Tyranny of Reality and the Autonomy of Painting* dating from 1989 and *Future Perspective, or why he's not the Man they say he is*, written in 1999, are both placed under the year 1989. The second text is a sequel to the first and is placed in relation to it, instead of chronologically under 1999.

4 In 1997 Dumas wrote the texts *Valentines Day* and *Always true*, especially for inclusion in the first edition, presented under the heading Epilogue. In this edition those texts have been placed as the last texts dating from the year 1997.

5 Two texts addressing the work of other artists in the first edition, *Goya the Fates* (1998) and *Bacon and Dumas, or the Discomfort of being 'coupled'* (Politics (of Art) 1995) have been maintained in their original positions.

Acknowledgements

Photo-courtesy
Studio Marlene Dumas, Amsterdam
Galerie Paul Andriesse, Amsterdam
Gallery Koyanagi, Tokyo
Kunsthalle Bern, Bern
Portikus, Frankfurt
Produzentengalerie, Hamburg
Zeno X, Antwerp
Frith Street Gallery, London
David Zwirner, New York

Photography
Paul Andriesse
Peter Cox
Gert-Jan van Rooij
and others

Grateful thanks to
Jan Andriesse
Rudolf Evenhuis
Jolie van Leeuwen

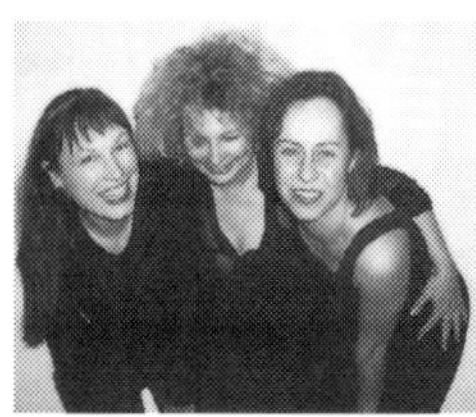

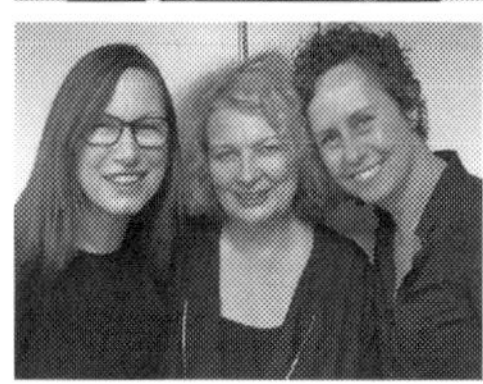

The designer, the writer and the editor 1998 / 2014

Colophon

Compilation & Editing | first and second edition
Mariska van den Berg
Marlene Dumas

Design, Layout & Typesetting | first and second edition
Gabriele Franziska Götz | ambulant design
Assistance
Mariska Gewald | second edition
Floor Koomen | first edition 1998

English translations | second edition 2014
Marlene Dumas
Yvette Rosenberg
English translations | first edition 1998
Marlene Dumas
Nicoline Gatehouse

Copyediting | second edition 2014
Selese Roche, who also advised on revising the first edition of 1998

Production
Printmanagement Plitt, Oberhausen

Published in North America by:
D.A.P./ Distributed Art Publishers
155 Sixth Avenue, Second Floor
New York City 10013-1507
www.artbook.com

A CIP record for this book is available from the Library of Congress

ISBN 978-1-938922-83-1

Front cover Marlene Dumas, *Silverplated* 1997
Back cover Marlene Dumas, *She Walks on Clouds* ca. 1990